A Spiritual Companion to
How to Get Along With Your Church

Beverly A. Thompson
Foreword by George B. Thompson, Jr.

The Pilgrim Press
Cleveland

Dedication

For George, whose wise, vulnerable writing gives hope to pastors like me,
even in the midst of much pain and struggle.
You, dear George, will always be my grace, my joy, my love!

The Pilgrim Press, 700 Prospect Avenue, Cleveland, Ohio 44115-1100,
thepilgrimpress.com
© 2006 Beverly A. Thompson

Biblical quotations are primarily from the New Revised Standard Version of the Bible. © 1989
by the Division of Christian Education of the National Council of the Churches of Christ in
the U.S.A., and are used by permission.

Printed in the United States of America on acid-free paper

10 09 08 07 06   5 4 3 2 1

Library of Congress Cataloging-in-Publication Data

Thompson, Beverly.
    A spiritual companion to How to get along with your church / Beverly A. Thompson;
    foreword, George B. Thompson, Jr.
      p. cm.
    ISBN 0-8298-1711-5
    1. Clergy—Prayer-books and devotions—English. 2. Pastoral theology—Meditations.
    I. Thompson, George B. (George Button), 1951– How to get along with your church.
    II. Title.
    BV4011.6.T46 2006
    253—dc22

                          2005028969

ISBN13 : 978-08298-1711-9
ISBN10 : 0-8298-1711-5

Contents

Foreword

For today's pastor, ministry is certainly no picnic. Oh, we read here and there —often to our private chagrin—of a new, fast-growing church somewhere that seems to have everything going for it. Americans love a winner, but many pastors these days feel more like losers coaching a losing team. The myth of success in our society does not encourage much honesty, even when your gut is telling you otherwise. So it is no small feat today for pastors—perhaps especially for pastors—to acknowledge that they could use some help. Tucked carefully away in many pastoral studies, partially hidden by rows of thick commentaries and preaching aids, rest those books by some other pastor who "made it," who now is telling the rest of us what it takes.

If pastors today could sit down together honestly and courageously, their stories would reveal a lot of *pain.* Most clergy whom I have met enter pastoral ministry because they sense a call from God. Just because you are "called," however, doesn't mean you are ready. Just because you are called doesn't mean you will be triumphant. Still, the Gospel ultimately deals with hope, and pastors want to believe that the pain they have experienced as pastors stands a chance of being transformed. Frustration, betrayal, resistance, weakness, loss of membership, board fights, leaking sanctuaries, bad decisions—indeed, for pastors, the pain is there and it is real. Pastors run into it, often naively and unexpectedly. This becomes the starting point for honesty. This is why pastors don't get along with their church.

Untreated, pain leads to *despair,* especially if it is not faced honestly. What will turn things around? What will offer pastors a way out of giving up? of coasting along? of abandoning their call? Beyond the pain of ministry that far too many pastors face eventually must emerge a new *conviction.* They must believe that things can be different, that "God makes a way out of no way," that when ministry gives you lemons, make holy lemonade. Pastors who are open to the new thing from God will discover a new way to approach their ministry. In my teaching, training, and writing, I am trying to stimulate this kind of new conviction—or at least a readiness for it. What happens when we discover that our pain is not a dead end? What happens when we begin to see things differently, through a new way that shows us the source of our pain? Then we can move, away from a preoccupation with the pain to a conviction about a new way.

I wrote *How to Get Along with Your Church* because of a conviction that pastors don't need to walk into the kind of pain that I went through as a pastor. I am not saying that pastoral ministry is a snap, only that pastors can be much better prepared. This is one of my deepest convictions. It is one that I try to share in all that I do.

In the practice of ministry, however, a conviction by itself is not worth much. If it is to count for Gospel ministry, conviction must lead to *enthusiasm.* I am not talking about superficial, whip-up-the-crowd motivation that quickly fades into a vague memory. Being enthusiastic—i.e., "in God"—in this sense means energized by the Holy Spirit. Good theology affirms that the divine breath blows in various ways to accomplish many things. Authentic spiritual enthusiasm does not come and go; it is a foundation for the life of faith, for those called together as Church.

How to Get Along with Your Church is a book born out of pain, conviction, and enthusiasm. So is this spiritual companion. Its author has written it out of her own pain as pastor, out of her conviction of a "new way," and out of her enthusiasm for sharing her gifts and knowledge creatively. I could not have written this book. I do not claim to be a spiritual director, which is one of Beverly's gifts. She is more sensitive than I am to the challenges of putting energy and focus to spiritual learning.

So this book will serve a valuable purpose. It walks the reader, one step at a time, one day at a time, through many key terms and main ideas from its source book. The exercises force you to slow down, to ponder, to focus, to hear what the Spirit might be trying to tell you about your church—and about yourself. Feel free to use the journaling space as you are prompted on each page. Moving words from heart to paper acts like a mirror: Even when we don't like what we see, at least we know what we are facing.

If you are reading this book, you probably don't need to be told "one more time" that things are changing. I have lived long enough to realize that even an idealist baby boomer like myself misses something of those elusive good ol' days. But the world does not stand still, and neither does God. As pastors, why should we learn how to get along with our church? Because that is where ministry can begin. I invite you, then, to take yourself on this journey—a journey of self-awareness, of spiritual growth, and of skill preparation. Gather up your pain, open up your new conviction, and discover your enthusiasm afresh! God is calling you ahead. Blessings in these travels!

GEORGE B. THOMPSON, JR.

Introduction

THE SECRET OF PASTORAL PAIN IS ONE OF the best-kept religious secrets ever. We clergy are the "called ones." We are viewed as people with all of the answers. Surely, God will grace us with beautiful, fulfilling ministries. Unfortunately, however, we know this is not reality. Over an eighteen-month period, in my presbytery, at least twelve pastors were forced out of calls or forced to leave congregations where they believed God wanted them to serve.

Michael was one of these pastors. It is because of Michael, and other clergy, even my own self, that I could not *not* write this book.

You see, like others of us who finally answer God's call into ministry in the midst of successful professional careers, Michael came to seminary from his golf-course home, dragging his wife and son into a tiny campus apartment. He had a very successful profession, but, like those fishermen of old, he left everything to follow Jesus.

In his first church following ordination, Michael was devoured by a church in decline. He did what they said they wanted him to do, but neither Michael nor his congregation had any idea of what was really going on. His leaving was pain-filled and left him with high blood pressure, depression, and despair.

Michael and his family still suffer; that church still suffers; and, Michael, like many other faithful pastors, will not go back into parish ministry. We live in a time in which pastoral leadership is under attack as churches themselves are in crisis. Pastors and church officials are struggling to find a way to better understand why things happen (or don't!) in their particular churches. Why is it that old patterns keep repeating themselves? Pastors do what they are called to do, often to the demise of their pastorates, just as happened to those pastors who served before them. My own pastoral experience has led me to look beyond the popular "family systems" model, to seek something that can help churches to grow strong and pastors to become leaders.

In the last ten years, I have served four churches, ranging from a large urban congregation to a small rural historic parish, a midsize suburban church to a stagnant church near a major educational and medical center. In all of these churches, I listened to what the church officers said they wanted to be and to do. I then sought to help them do what they said they wanted. In one of these churches, only after experiencing great pain, did I discover that a very small cadre within the congregation had its own agenda. It seemed determined to use its dominating power to keep the church the way they wanted it to be—even if that meant jeopardizing its future. I was very familiar with family systems theory as a tool for analysis and intervention because of my training and experience as a pastoral counselor. Though I practiced and taught this theory to my parishioners, I came to sense that something was missing.

During those same years of parish ministry, I watched and listened as other ministers struggled with their church situations. At first, I didn't give it much thought: I assumed that the problems were created by the pastors themselves. They must not be capable enough or able to separate their identity from their work. It was not until I had gone through my own pastoral pain that I began to see things differently. Now I believe that this scenario of deep confusion and pain is common among pastors who are trying to lead their congregations through necessary, faithful, but difficult change. Furthermore, I am quite concerned that clergy who leave pastorates under a cloud lose their energy and sense of calling.

Once I read *How to Get Along with Your Church,* I realized that a cultural approach to congregations answers many of my questions about the many dynamics between pastor and congregation. While I was learning to use this new model, I realized that I would do better if I had daily support. On any given day, I would walk into my office and be barraged by the same old issues—church members wanting easy, fast answers that would not work in the long run. Luckily for me, I could pick up my phone and get encouragement directly from the book's author, my husband. He coached me through specific situations, guiding me time and time again to conceptual insights from his book and showing me how those insights lead to a different way of handling things.

It is because of this turning-point experience in my own pastoral experience that I believe *How to Get Along with Your Church* indeed offers a groundbreaking model. It provides a new paradigm for church leaders that can make a difference in the life of their churches. Within the past year, I have joined my husband in training and coaching pastors and lay leaders of a number of churches. Participants come away from the training with excitement, hope, and a new wisdom about the work to be done in their particular churches.

However, because this new model does involve a shift in paradigm, the actual work of learning and applying it is far from simple. Though a pastor may believe he or she has "got it," it is easy to become discouraged when confronted with parishioners who are not willing to learn or who want quick and easy answers. When we are under prolonged stress, we tend to act out of familiar internal patterns, not necessarily helpful ones. In our ministry of coaching and training church officers, George and I have sensed the potential for having a resource that gives daily spiritual support because, as they learn to apply new ideas faithfully, pastors, deacons, and elders also need grounding. In particular, pastors need fresh ways of relating their daily work to their own faith and capacity to lead. They can benefit from tangible, guided practices. With such resources, pastors can become aware in new ways of the Spirit of God in their midst, ready to transform as they learn.

One way to strengthen this kind of learning process is to encourage the learner to keep a journal. In this spiritual companion, I have included written "prompts" and space on the pages for daily journaling. In my work as a spiritual director with clergy and lay persons, I know both the value and struggle of daily journaling. *Over and over again, people tell me that they just don't know how to begin.* Over and over again, they ask me for daily triggers or specific practices designed to help them get started. Besides these prompts, I also have included here a variety of prayers, songs, words, and suggested rituals. These can spiritually nurture and encourage those who use this book. Pastors and lay members who become learners are better equipped to lead their congregations.

This companion offers you one hundred days of guidance, a disciplined way to ponder and apply insights from *How to Get Along with Your Church.* In the following pages, you will find quotations from the book, along with page references. They will be helpful for referring back to a particular section during your meditation time to help you intentionally focus on one insight throughout the day. Beyond the references themselves, the journal space and the spiritual thoughts are designed for one purpose: they help you to create a sacred space for doing holy work. Yielding yourself to the Holy Spirit's instruction is the beginning of wisdom, and today's churches need as much wisdom as they can get.

I invite you to walk with me on a pastoral journey of self-discovery and preparation. Set aside your sacred space; fill it with your Bible, a journal and pen, and even a small bowl of water. Enter it daily and be prepared to meet your Companion. It is my earnest prayer that you will "get along with your church." God intends for the life that you share with them to bear fruit in the name of the Lord.

DAY 1

"I Thought I Knew…"

How well do you know what you are getting into? (Page 1)

IF YOU ARE LIKE MOST PASTORS, you earnestly thought you knew what the congregation you are serving was like when you answered God's call to serve them. Something has opened your eyes and now you know that you really don't know. The good news is that you are ready to find out!

So, on this day one of your journey of learning, take a breath and close your eyes once more. Remember your hopes and excitement as well as your fears as you began your pastorate with this particular congregation. Sit with those memories as you pray this prayer written by a fellow pilgrim, Thomas Merton:

> O Lord, I have no idea where I am going, I do not see the road ahead of me. I cannot know for certain where it will end. Nor do I really know myself, and the fact that I think I am following your will does not mean that I am actually doing so. But I believe that the desire to please you does in fact please you. And I hope I have that desire in all that I am doing.
>
> I hope that I will never do anything apart from that desire. And I know that, if I do this, you will lead me by the right road, though I may know nothing about it. Therefore, I will trust you always though I may seem to be lost and in the shadow of death I will not fear, for you are ever with me and you will never leave me to face my perils alone.[1]

Now, write five of those hopes and fears in your journal, and offer them to God.

_____

_____

_____

_____

_____

_____

_____

DAY 2

What Am I Afraid of in Nineveh?

The danger in any new pastorate is that the pastor will not relate strongly enough to the culture of that particular church community. (Page 2)

JONAH IS NOT THE ONLY CALLED ONE who is so frustrated with a people that he doesn't even want to offer them a grace-filled word from God. Wounded pastors are no different. Many of us just want out. We want to run from the Church and from this thing called—ministry, only to discover that God does not give up on us so easily. Over and over again God calls us to serve. If we are not afraid of learning, we can gather some new tools, and when we get to that Nineveh we will be better prepared to understand and relate to the culture of the congregation as, together, we experience God's grace.

As you prepare for this day of learning to better understand the culture of your congregation, sit and pray through these words from *Angels in America.*

> The angel has come to the character Prior who is infected with the AIDS virus. Prior protests that he is no prophet, just a sick lonely man. The response comes from God: "You can't run from your occupation, Jonah. Hiding from me one place, you will find me in another."[2]
>
> —Tony Kushner, Theatre Communications Group, New York

As you journal this morning, offer to God your running and your places of hiding.

_____

_____

_____

_____

_____

_____

_____

DAY 3

Lookin' For Love in All the Wrong Places

What you see is not what you get. (Page 4)

By now you have learned that the Church Profile, resumé, or information form may have given you statistics and some words you wanted to hear but little more. Sometimes we pastors say "yes" to a call because we are really looking to be loved by a congregation. And, yes, we are looking to love them, too. So what's going on here?

This morning as you begin to think intentionally about your particular congregation, begin with the obvious. Take a deep breath, open wide your arms, then close your eyes. Bring to mind the objects, rituals, and structures that are easily observable in your particular congregation.

As you see in your mind's eye, offer each artifact to God, praying:

O God, I see _____, I give thanks for _____ and I wonder what that really means.

At the conclusion of this prayer, write what you "saw" and what you have "heard" that these artifacts mean.

_____

_____

_____

_____

_____

_____

_____

DAY 4

Am I Willing to Learn to Earn Cultural Capital?

Paul earned the right to be heard. (Page 3)

As pastor of this church, you are seeing that you have some things to learn about the culture of your congregation. Developing cultural capital takes time and intentionality. Remember, you are choosing to earn cultural capital in order to help your church discover God's call. In addition, you are also earning cultural capital so that you really can get along with your church.

In these quiet moments ask yourself:

What is my purpose as pastor of this congregation?

What persons or group(s) act as roadblocks for my ideas or projects?

With which three persons I could sit in my quest to discover key culture bearers?

As you sit in silence for a few moments praying through these questions, pray through Paul's words found in 1 Corinthians 9:22: "I have become all things to all people, that I might by all means serve some."

Write three ways in which you can begin to build cultural capital in your congregation today. As you write each way, offer it to God.

_____

_____

_____

_____

_____

_____

_____

_____

○●○

DAY 5

We are a Warm and Friendly Church

. . . espoused values, what the community says it values. (Page 7)

I HAVE OFTEN WONDERED WHY Christians so enjoy Halloween. We don't
believe in monsters and ghosts but we love to create masks and costumes
for our children (and sometimes for ourselves). My cynical side says it's
because we churchgoing folk are so used to wearing masks; hiding what
we really think, it's just natural that Halloween overshadows All Saints'
Day. Most congregations really think they are warm and friendly, but are
they really hiding?

This morning sit and contemplate what you hear your parishioners say
about themselves, the artifacts, and the ministry and mission of the
church. Jot down the following: five things the congregation says about
itself, and five things it says about what it wants from a pastor. When you
have finished writing, invite God to sit with you. As you and God sit in
silence, ask God to help you take off your mask so that your parishioners
might experience grace as well.

_____

_____

_____

_____

_____

_____

_____

_____

DAY 6

It's Not Easy Being Green—
Kermit the Frog

*Shared basic assumptions are not easy to determine
but they define the culture. (Page 8)*

BY NOW YOU HAVE LOTS OF THINGS stirring in your pastoral identity. You
see things. You hear things. Still, you find yourself bumping into things
like a kid in the dark.

In order to get along with your church, you need to understand what
is going on in the deepest layer of its culture. As I worked to learn this new
model, I found myself feeling greener and greener. Like Kermit the Frog,
I was not so sure I wanted to know anything else at all. After all, it's not
easy being green!

As you begin to meditate on the shared assumptions that lie deep within your congregation, take a deep breath, sing Kermit's song, then close
your eyes. Think about all the things you are still "green" about—things
you thought you knew, things you know that you don't understand.

You may still be green, but you are beginning to grow wise.

In your journal today, offer God your greenness as you note words and
phrases that remind you of your naiveté *and* the ways that being green are
helping you discover more about the culture of your particular congregation.

_____

_____

_____

_____

_____

_____

_____

○●○

DAY 7

Something Called "Swamp-Talk"

Artifacts (Page 9)

IT TAKES TIME TO UNDERSTAND the culture of your congregation. It is just too important to miss. What are the basic shared assumptions that lay beneath what the congregation says is important (espoused values) and how the congregation behaves and constructs objects?

> Think of your congregation as a swamp.
> What do you see when you look at the shoreline? (Artifacts)
> What do you see when you look into the water? (Espoused values)
> Now, are you ready to begin looking into that mucky water to see what's in the mud? [3]

In your journal this morning, sketch your swamp. Fill in the blanks as you can. Sit with it. Now, offer your swamp to God. Ask God to help you discover three deeply held shared assumptions (stuff in the mud!) this week.

P.S. Remember, you cannot name the stuff in the mud. Your parishioners will have to share them with you, and it will take time for them to say them out loud! Just keep singing, and praying.

_____

_____

_____

_____

_____

_____

_____

DAY 8

It Takes All the Layers to Make a Swamp Work!

Artifacts, espoused values and deeply held assumptions. (Page 9)

AS YOU CONTINUE TO LOOK AT THE "ecosystem" of your church's swamp, do not fall into the trap of thinking that any of the parts are bad. Remember:

> Swamps need what is on the shore (artifacts that can be seen).
> Swamps need what is in the water (espoused values that say what things mean).
> Swamps need mud and all that is in it (deeply held shared assumption).

As you continue to look deeply into the mud of your church's swamp, remember that the ecosystem of your church needs all the parts to function. In your prayer journal, continue to offer to God what you are beginning to see on the shore, in the water, and in the mud. Give thanks to God for each of these, and sit quietly as you begin to discipline yourself to give value to what is best or right for your congregation as you explore the swamp in all of its beauty.

_____

_____

_____

_____

_____

_____

_____

_____

DAY 9

Layers of Culture

Besides thinking of congregations in levels, it is helpful for us to be aware that it also exists in layers. (Page 11)

Coffee, Tea and French Croissant—
Flaky, tasty, yet hard to hold onto.

THIS MORNING AS YOU OFFER God your "time of learning," peel back the layers of your congregation's context. What are its symbols of macroculture? Can you begin to name its artifacts, its espoused values? What are the deep underlying assumptions about its macroculture that shape the congregation's life?

As you prepare to pray and journal this morning, offer to God how this layer appeals to you. It is too crusty, too flaky, bitter, sweet, tough…? Sit with these thoughts and then jot them in your journal as your morning offering.

_____

_____

_____

_____

_____

_____

_____

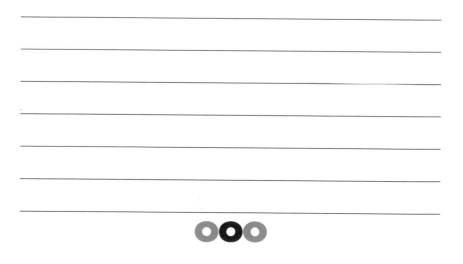

DAY 10

Why Me, Lord?

BY NOW YOU MAY BE A BIT FRUSTRATED, or just plain tired of trying to figure it out. Learning a new way of understanding is not easy. It takes time
and intentionality. The cry has come from prophets throughout the cen-
turies. Yet, you are reminded this day that you are not alone in your learning. God's Spirit is forever present. God is reliable and faithful.

Take a deep breath and pray this prayer.

Why me Lord,
>Why in the middle of this mixed up, chaotic world did you come
>calling on me?
>I don't know how to please them and you,
>I move a step forward and get pushed three steps back.
>Even the simple task of understanding what they really mean causes
>confusion.
>Why me Lord, why now??? Amen.

Cry out your "whys" to God as you journal this morning.

_____

_____

_____

_____

_____

_____

DAY 11

Still Noticing

It is the reality of the confluence of cultural streams that makes church analysis possible—albeit subtle and challenging. (Page 20)

TEN DAYS . . . BY NOW YOU ARE LOOKING all around you and noticing things you've not noticed before. You are noticing that your church is much more than the folks you see on any given Sunday. And, you are noticing that few of those folks have begun to notice the streams of culture that are converging at the door.

Today as you intentionally notice the ways in which the streams of culture converge upon your church, imagine a simple sketch, with your church at the center and the various streams of culture that you are noticing flowing toward it. Then sit in silence with these "noticings."

After a period of silence, offer them to God with your questions and your anxieties, even as you pray this prayer:

We are well-schooled in the affirmation that you are Holy Other and you are completely unlike us. And it is your unlikeness that is the ground of your capacity to save us. Now that we are surrounded and noticing, as we have never noticed, that our neighbors all around us are holy other, so unlike us and in a variety of ways that issues invitation and assault to us. So we pray for your mercy that comes out of your otherness that we may learn to be at ease and in love with those who are other than us, whereby, perhaps, to be healed in our own strange otherness. We pray in the otherly name of Jesus. Amen.

Walter Brueggeman[4]

_____

_____

_____

_____

_____

_____

◐●◑

DAY 12

Water, Water Everywhere . . .

When you are preparing to enter a congregation for the first time,
you are walking into a stream of culture that is created out of
many other streams. (Page 20)

IF YOU HAVE TRULY BEGUN TO PAY ATTENTION to the culture of your congregation, you may be the only one who is becoming aware of the converging streams: levels of culture, layers of culture, ways of understanding the makeup of your church in its particular community. It is likely that you feel isolated in your new learnings, somewhat like one alone in the wilderness. Today, as you continue to observe the confluence of the streams into your church, carry with you the prophetic words of Isaiah 43:

"I give water in the wilderness . . . to my chosen people . . . so that they [in community] might declare my praise. . . ."

As you sit with your new learnings, begin to name the streams flowing into the wilderness of your church. One by one, offer them to God in written prayer in this journal as you pray, over and over again, the words of the prophet.

_____

_____

_____

_____

_____

_____

_____

_____

DAY 13

Can You Hear What I Hear?

American society continues to be deeply infused by a way of life that is by nature primarily oral. (Page 17)

AS PASTOR OF A RURAL CONGREGATION, my first Vacation Bible School was one of my least favorite experiences in ministry. Night after night I grimaced as the children were taught to recite verses from the Bible (most often using non-inclusive texts from the King James translation). I was convinced that it was more important to understand what the text "meant" than to spit out scripture word for word. How I wish I had read Tex Sample's book[5] or understood the importance of traditional orality in mesoculture.

Do you remember the old, old song: "Tell me the stories of Jesus, I long to hear. . . . ?"As you prepare to move into this new day, what is a story that lives in your particular congregation that continues to annoy your "educated self"? What part of your church's mesoculture values this story? What is it about the story that disconnects you?

Sit with it for awhile, then offer your thoughts to God in written prayer, grateful that God connects our stories, making them sacred.

DAY 14

Take a Long, Loving Look at the Real

Why would anyone want to join us? (Page 19)

FOR MOST PROTESTANTS, CONTEMPLATION is an edgy word. It brings to mind Paul's being "caught up to the third heaven" (2 Corinthians 12:2) or monks silently meditating in isolation.

Steven Wirth of the Center for Contemplative Dialogue[6] suggests that contemplative dialogue begins with taking a "long, loving look at the real." Real means just that. In order for your church to discover "why would anyone want to join us," it must look contemplatively at its whole self, taking a long, loving look at what is real.

As you sit with God this morning, make two columns in your journal. In the first column, offer three realities of your congregation. In the second column, list three reasons why someone might be attracted (or unattracted) to a church with those three realities. As you pray in this way, take your own long, loving look at the real in each of the three. Notice the assumptions you place on each. Pay attention to your feelings. Do not analyze, describe or criticize. Just take this morning to look.

> Take a long,
> > Loving,
> > > Look
> > > > At the Real
> > And, you will find the holy in the depth.

COLUMN ONE	COLUMN TWO
_____	_____
_____	_____
_____	_____
_____	_____
_____	_____
_____	_____

DAY 15

Shock Waves

One of the first key tactics is to recognize conflict just as it begins to surface. (Page 107)

IF SOME OF THE KEY CULTURE-BEARERS in one of the subcultures of your church have begun to notice that you are beginning to figure out some things about the congregation's culture, and if they perceive a threat to their way of life, you may be experiencing the early signs of shockwaves— conflict! Remember, weakening congregations can become "shockingly irrational."

As you become more intentional in learning your congregation's culture, you will begin to notice how certain people want what they want—

now. They will be unwilling to learn, to bend, to dream. When this reality appears, shockwaves begin to reverberate through the congregation. You are now aware that this is one sign that your church is weakening on the life-cycle model. It appears strong, but it is brittle. Old assumptions are deeply held by some, and now that they are coming to the surface, the shockwaves are beginning to be felt throughout the congregation. What you are learning can be perceived as a threat to some of your members. Stay with it. Keep reframing the issues, and keep the question before you and them:

"What does this say about our church at this time?"

This morning, offer God your anxieties and your learnings, even as the shockwaves begin to make you tremble.

_____

_____

_____

_____

_____

_____

_____

_____

DAY 16

Are You One of Us?

What adoption does not mean. (Page 37)

A WISE OLDER PASTOR ONCE SUGGESTED that I watch out for those folks in the church who did the most for me. He was right when he said that they wanted me.

To control me.

To own me.

Being adopted by a congregation is a delicate balance of living in the midst and still on the edge. You will know when you have moved from the edge too close to the midst when you find yourself in the midst of, and siding with, a subculture. Marginality is a tool that connects you with your congregation but gives you a wider, more purposeful vision of the whole rather than a part.

As you sit in silence for a moment this morning, begin to name those persons or families within your congregation who spend much time and energy with you. What subculture do these persons represent? Could they bias your opinion or pull you into their circle? Name these persons in your prayer as you seek God's guidance in being with them and yet staying marginal.

DAY 17

Land Mines

What gets us into trouble . . . . (Page 7)

I CAN STILL REMEMBER THAT Sunday morning when Martha came running into my study before worship. On the verge of tears she whimpered, "The flowers are not here." Okay, I thought. Surely one Sunday morning we can worship without flowers. Sensing her anxiety, I decided to walk into the sanctuary with her so that I could reassure her that we could "get away without flowers this one time and speak with the florist on Monday."

To my surprise, right in front of the pulpit sat a huge vase of flowers. "What's this?" I asked. Her answer was surprising: "These are not the flowers that Milton's family ordered. They ordered two identical arrangements, just like always. We cannot disappoint them."

I suggested we take the vase and divide it into two arrangements. Before I could blink, Martha had the vase in her arms and the florist's home phone number. I had no idea what this artifact symbolized in the shared assumptions of this congregation. Clearly, I had just missed stepping on another landmine!

This morning as you sit in this silent space, think of the "landmines" you have run into in your church and begin to journal them as you offer them to God. Take a bit more time and jot a thought about what you learned about the artifacts, espoused values, and shared assumptions of your congregation in these situations.

Sit in silence after sharing your offering with God. When you are ready, join with our brothers and sisters whose landmines come in the forms of addiction and pray the Serenity Prayer:

God grant me the serenity to accept the things I cannot change, the courage to change what can be changed, and the wisdom to know the difference. Amen.

_____

_____

_____

_____

_____

_____

_____

○●○

DAY 18

Maybe Somebody Else Can Do This

Still struggling with land mines. (Page 7)

YOU ARE DOING IMPORTANT WORK, and it is far from easy. On stressful, busy days (which seems to apply to all the days pastors give to their ministry), you may feel that somebody else can do this better than you. You are not alone. We all feel that way one day or another.

Give yourself space with God today as you read the words of Annie Dillard:

> Who shall ascend to the hill of the Lord? Or who shall stand for us in his holy place? There is no one but us. There is no one to send, nor a clean hand, nor a pure heart on the face of the earth, nor in the earth, but only us, a generation comforting ourselves with the notion that we have come at an awkward time, that our innocent fathers are all dead—as if innocence had ever been—and our children busy and troubled, and we ourselves unfit, not yet ready, having each of us chosen wrongly, made a false start, failed, yielded to impulse and the tangled comfort of pleasures, and grown exhausted, unable to seek the thread, weak and involved. But, there is no one but us. There never has been.[7]

As you sit with God, journal your prayer remembering who and whose you are.

_____

_____

_____

_____

_____

_____

_____

○●○

DAY 19

Help! I Need a Road Map

All organizations in our era must account for the what, the who,
the how and the why of their existence. (Page 83)

BEGIN YOUR MORNING REMEMBERING that you are called by God to lead
and to learn. The work you are undertaking is ministry at its very core.
Begin your prayer this morning by praying, again, the prayer written by
Thomas Merton on Day 1. After praying the prayer, ask God to help you
discern the following functions of your church.

As you write what you are learning, think about the tug-of-war competing among the functions within your congregation. Draw lines where
the tugs are occurring today. Then sit with God and begin to see your road
map.

What

_____

_____

_____

Who

_____

_____

_____

How

_____

_____

_____

Why

_____

_____

_____

○●○

DAY 20

That's Just What We Do!

Perform (Page 84)

AS YOU BEGIN TO STRUGGLE WITH THE "what" function of your congregation, pay attention to what you hear said about what your church does. Churches do things. But is your congregation doing what it does because you want it to, because it always has, or as a result of its sense of vision?

This morning as you center yourself in silence, think about what your church is doing and why. In your prayer journal note three of these activities or programs. Beside each one, write where the time and energy is spent. Sit awhile with these thoughts. Then offer the "what" of your church to God:

Ever Creating and Re-creating God,
Your church is busy.
Your people struggle with trying to do more and be more,
And yet, we find ourselves scattered and less than vital.
Accept what we do to your glory.
Create space for me to notice,
Create space for me to listen,
Create space for me to understand,
So that I might make a difference and lead them into your vision.
Amen.

_____

_____

_____

_____

_____

DAY 21

Who are We Anyway?

But, it also has to do with the sense of belonging. . . . (Page 84)

THIS MORNING, AS YOU CONSIDER THE "who" of your church, think not only about the people who make up the congregation but also the community around you. How related are the members to the community? What does it take to become "one of us"?

Take your journal and begin to write the groupings of people who make up the "who" of your church. Now close your eyes and see their faces. Offer the "who" to God. Throughout the rest of the day pay attention to the relatedness of your church to the people of the community.

_____

_____

_____

⦾⚫⦾

DAY 22

But, We've Always Done It That Way

How?—Execute (Page 84)

As you continue to help your church gain, regain, or retain its vitality, you will want to look at how it gets things done. How are decisions made? Who carries the power and authority to get things done?

This morning, sit awhile and remember the last major decision that was made in your church. Who was involved? What group or person actually made it happen? If conflict was part of the decision, whose voice was heard? Whose voice was ignored? Notice your feelings about this process.

Offer your understandings (and your questions) to the Spirit this morning as you write them in your prayer journal.

_____

_____

_____

_____

_____

_____

_____

_____

DAY 23

Does God Still Call Congregations Today?

Why do we do what we do as a church? (Page 85)

EVERY CHURCH HAS TO HAVE A REASON TO EXIST, and it is not to be a social club, right?

Unfortunately, few churches are serious about identifying a clear and compelling vision, and the focus remains on how can we get things done, not why. Decisions about the other functions fall into place when churches look at their visions for guidance.

In *Futuring Your Church: Finding Your Vision and Making It Work,* George B. Thompson, Jr., reminds us of God's intentional call to congregations.[8]

This morning as you invite God to sit with you, offer in your prayer journal your thoughts as to why your church is being called today. How can you help your congregation listen and claim the call, the vision? Ask God to help you lead your congregation in a time of discernment. Envision your church's call as part of a journey, looking ahead, not just behind.

_____

_____

_____

_____

_____

_____

_____

OOO

DAY 24

What Next?

Leading toward vitality. (Page 85)

PASTORS WHO ARE LEADERS PUT THEIR ENERGY into helping their congregations keep why, what, who, and how in creative relationship. Vital, dynamic churches will need to get there, or get back there, before they can learn how to stay there.

Pastors do ministry when you help your congregation keep a vision before them in all that they do.

As you sit in silence this morning, invite God to help you see where your church is putting its focus: who, what, how, why. As you read the words from the Prophet Habakkuk (Habakkuk 2:1–3), ask God to help you stand watch and wait until the right time so that you can wisely lead your congregation in writing and living God's vision. Offer your intentions to God in your prayer journal.

_____

_____

_____

_____

_____

_____

_____

_____

DAY 25

What You Hear is Not What They Mean!

Something deeper is at stake. (Page 53)

TODAY IS A GOOD DAY TO LOOK CLOSELY at the artifacts in and around your church.

You probably think you know what they mean to this particular congregation. After all, you've seen them before in other churches you have served. Be careful! Something deeper may be at stake. Pastors who are leaders not only listen to what is said, but they also take time to discover underlying assumptions about the espoused values.

As you seek God's guidance today, think about the artifacts you have noticed.

If you have a flag, what does that say about the deeper assumption of war? Does the sanctuary have artificial, fresh, or no flowers? How old is the hymnal? Which class has the "big" room for Sunday school? What other artifacts seem to say something that you need to look at more closely? Journal your thoughts as your prayer to the One who knows us and our churches—completely.

_____

_____

_____

_____

_____

_____

_____

DAY 26

Still Looking for Vitality?

Pastors who are leaders . . . . (Page 86)

IF YOU ARE STILL LOOKING FOR WAYS to help your church move to (or remain!) in the vital, dynamic stage of the life cycle, remember this: Pastors who are leaders put their energy into helping their congregations keep "why, what, who, and how" in creative relationships.

Keeping the four-function model in mind, sit for a few moments and invite God to be present with you as you pay attention to the what, the who, the how, and the why of your church's existence. Journal your thoughts as you offer them to God.

_____

_____

_____

_____

_____

_____

_____

DAY 27

Power and Voicelessness

"Our secrets stay that way." (Page 101)

REV. JONES IS NOT THE ONLY ONE of us who did not understand the importance placed on saving face over public exposure. One Sunday morning in a rural community after baptizing a young child, I moved to the communion table and began the prayer of thanksgiving over the elements. Little did I know that right behind me in the choir, another young child was being dragged by the neck by his grandfather to the top of the choir loft. I knew nothing of the struggle or of the one woman who tried to stop the man. We celebrated the sacrament. Familiar hugs and greetings were exchanged at the door. Photos were taken of the baptized child at the font with his new pastor. And the choir director, an elder, and I went to lunch together. Nothing was said about the turmoil that occurred during the prayer.

Imagine my shock when I went into the local bank the next morning and was greeted by the vice president whose wife was the woman who tried to "save" the child. He took me into his office and recounted the event and their great concern for the child. Not one other member of this congregation ever spoke of it. And the loving woman and her husband could say little in public for obvious reasons. Of course, they asked me to speak to the grandfather, which I did. His response was clear: "None of your business."

Although I did speak with social services, their response was much the same.

Whose voice could not be heard?

Where was the power and how was it being used?

To whom would you turn in your congregation?

Write your thoughts as you sit and offer them to God, remembering with the psalmist that you and your congregation are not alone in such struggles.

O God, you do know me.
You know what I do and what I think;
  I have no secrets from you.
You find me on whatever path I choose,
and you hold me close, very close.
Thank you.

DAY 28

Return to the Edge of the Swamp!

Marginality—being able to stand at times on the edges.
(Page 80)

By now you are doing more than just noticing the artifacts and listening to the espoused values within your congregation. You may think you have uncovered those deeply shared assumptions that lie deep in the mud of the swamp of your church, but have your church's session, board, deacons, or other key culture-bearers begun to name those assumptions? Remember, the work is theirs to do.

As you prepare to sit with God and think through the swamp again this morning, turn back to the drawing you made on Day Seven. Look at it carefully. Take time to add new insights to it, including what others have named on these three levels of the swamp.

Do you find yourself judgmental in looking deeply into the swamp of your church?

Are your own espoused values for Christian life and faith compatible with those of this congregation? If not, you may be feeling worn out. Pay attention to your feelings of fatigue and frustration. Remember, you must be outside of the church's culture in order to keep learning.

Now close your eyes and begin to breathe slowly. See the swamp of your church.

Drag yourself out of the mud. Take another deep breath. Sit for a moment and, with your eyes closed, see what is around you. Now stand up and open your eyes. Ask God to walk around the shore with you. Pray aloud what you see, offering each thing you see to God without judgment.

With your arms wide open, imagine the shoreline again. See it vividly. Step on the edge. You are experiencing marginality. Remember the feeling!

_____

_____

_____

_____

_____

_____

_____

DAY 29

Help, I Need Somebody!

Know thyself. (Page 118)

IT IS IRONIC THAT WE WHO DO SO MUCH pastoral counseling take such poor care of our own spiritual and emotional selves. Life as a pastor is filled with joy, struggle, and a whole lot of stress. Even Jesus called folks to help him. As you continue to learn more about how to get along with your church, it is time to find ways to take care of yourself as well.

In the chaos of the church, we pastors need friends and colleagues outside of our congregations, outside of our vocations—people we can trust to support and nurture us.

Name one person you would like to become your support and pray this day that you make time to build a trusting relationship with him or her. As you contemplate marginality, journal this person's name as your prayer of need to God.

_____

_____

_____

_____

_____

_____

_____

DAY 30

What Kind of Love is This?

Christians don't fight. (Page 100)

YOU AND I know that churches are the place where many folks choose to fight, and that fighting is far from Christ-like. For some people, church is the only place they have power. For others, fear of changing what feels right gives some sort of power to do whatever is necessary to keep things the way they are (or were).

Understanding the "triggered assumptions," such as "Christians don't fight," "Pastors don't fight," "We decide how much power the pastor has," will help pastors stay on the margins and form cultural strategies to help churches move successfully through conflict. Rather than allowing ourselves to be pulled into the fray, we must ask the question over and over again: "What does this say about our church at this time?"

As you take this quiet time apart from the world this morning, be reminded that even Jesus had to stand up against the evil-doings in the church. Paul's letters are filled with dealings with troubled congregants. In every denomination, pastors struggle to find sanity in the midst of the conflict.

As you sit in prayer this morning, offer to God three things that attempt to pull you into the center of conflict. Pay attention to your feelings as you write these in your journal.

After each thing respond to the attempt with the question: "What does this say about our church at this time?"

_____

_____

_____

_____

_____

_____

_____

DAY 31

Cross-Bearing and Resurrection

Like a machine, we replace our defective parts. (Page 103)

I STILL FEEL GUILTY THAT I DIDN'T KNOW about George's book, *How to Get Along with Your Church*, when working with seminary interns. I watched them grow into their pastoral identities. I celebrated their calls to small congregations in deep decline. And now, I see far too many of those "called ones" no longer willing to be crucified, no longer able to serve God in churches. A few hung on for a couple of calls. At least one of those second-career pastors now struggles with depression and high blood pressure. The family he pulled away from a professional environment and a lovely home now struggles for survival.

If I had only had the tools you are learning, I would have shared them, but it is too late. The damage is done. Resurrection comes to those faithful ones by grace alone, and I grieve for the churches who so need their pastoral leadership

You, too, may be experiencing what feels like death, but if you stay on the margin and keep learning and using these tools, resurrection is on its way for you and your congregation. I have watched it happen.

As you sit in silence for a few moments, notice the weight of your arms as they hang at your side. Drop your head and notice the tension in your neck and shoulders. Slowly breathe out the struggle. Envision it leaving your tired, anxious body.

Now open wide your arms as you take in new breath. Experience the Spirit breathing into you life, hope, resurrection. Offer your resurrection breath to God and when you are ready, write in your journal a few descriptive words about your cross-bearing. Now write your prayer for resurrection.

_____

_____

_____

_____

_____

_____

_____

_____

ooo

DAY 32

It's Too Easy to Forget

Know thyself. (Page 118)

WE PASTORS GET SO TIED UP IN WHAT we need to do to follow Christ's call that we don't often listen to scripture that just might offer us some much-needed comfort. In fact, we just may forget the words of Jesus that offer us the support and courage we so need to be faithful in our calling. Yes, we are called to baptize and make disciples, but Jesus didn't stop talking there.

Today as you continue your quest to learn what you need in order to get along with your church, pray the words of Jesus found in what we call

"The Great Commission" (Matthew 28:19–20). In your journal prayer, write five ways you might experience Jesus as you continue to follow his call.

_____

_____

_____

_____

_____

_____

_____

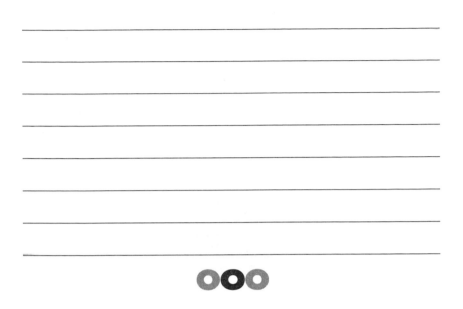

DAY 33

Pentecost: The Gift of Ears!

Attention to the stories, and to the telling of them, alerts the new pastor to some of the congregation's espoused values. (Page 35)

WE CHRISTIANS LIKE TO CLAIM Pentecost as the birthday of the Church because on that day people from all over were filled with the Spirit. Even though they spoke in varied languages, they were able to understand one another's words. Much has been made about this gift of tongues, but little about the gift of ears (Acts 2: 1–8).

Today as you continue to dig deeply into the culture of your congregation, listen with "ears of the Spirit." Hear more than words in the stories of the people. Pay attention to their sayings. Be intentional. Use their sayings and words in your sermons. Let your people know you have "ears to hear."

As you prepare for this day, be intentional about listening to those you meet.

Close your eyes as you open your ears and your heart to God. Notice the sounds around you. Jot them in your journal.

Now think of the "sayings" you hear frequently within your congregation and its community. Write them in your journal and listen for them today. Offer your "hearings to God."

DAY 34

Empty?

Recovering for a Reason. (Page 59)

IN REV. BRUCE'S CASE, it was the "being present with" a community that gained him the trust and respect of the people. He honored their values and assumptions and thus developed cultural capital. For many of us that takes much time, much energy, and many failures.

In a church I served, I gave much of my pastoral energy to a family whose young daughter was diagnosed with an inoperable brain tumor. The congregation seemed to rally around this family as well. But, as this situation lingered, some "squabbling" was whimpered by one or two in a dominant subculture. It was quiet, but it gained its own jealous voice.

I became disillusioned and disappointed. The contradiction between values and professed prayer on top of long hours of presence took their toll. Like at least a few of you, I found myself empty. In order to stay in touch with our calling, we need intentional reminders and support. We need to replenish our buckets with "rivers of living water." "And let the one who believes in me drink. As the scripture has said, 'Out of the believer's heart shall flow rivers of living water'" (John 7:38).

Today as you sit in silence, remember the names of persons you listed in this journal a few days ago. Have you created time to be in touch with at least one of them?

As you continue commune with God, write down three ways you will begin to refill, refresh, and renew as you drink of the Spirit's waters.

_____

_____

_____

_____

_____

_____

_____

_____

○○●○

DAY 35

They Look Like the Church I Just Served . . .

The learning pastor . . . (Page 79)

OKAY, NOW, WHAT YOU'VE THOUGHT for a while has been validated. You cannot trust what you read on a church information form or in an interview. Churches mean well, but they are as uncertain as you are about what they really want and need. Comforting? I doubt it.

Remind yourself that what you are learning now will render you capable of entering a congregation and learning its culture before you do anything to help it change.

Just be careful. If you forget and find yourself thinking that they look like the church you served before, that they worship like the church you served before, that they need what the church you served before needs—then take a deep breath and look deep into the swamp!

Today, as you continue to learn how to get along with your church, slow down.

Remember, it is good to keep looking, to keep asking the questions. As you think of the ways your church is like another you have served or known, in your prayer journal, compare what you are learning about the culture there and how that makes a difference compare in your prayer journal.

_____

_____

_____

_____

_____

_____

_____

DAY 36

Wade in the Water

A parish's richness and depth begin with its three levels of culture. (Page 92)

BEFORE YOU BEGIN THIS MORNING, bring a small bowl of water into your space.

As you continue to wade in the water of your congregation's culture, remember you cannot name or change their particular shared basic assumptions. The best you can do is to wade in the water with them.

As you make this old spiritual your prayer for this time, look into your bowl of water.

Dip your fingers into the water. Making the sign of the cross on your own forehead, remember that you, TOO, have been claimed in the waters of baptism as God's beloved.

"Wade in the water, wade in the water, children; wade in the water; Lord, don't you trouble the water."

"Wade in the water, wade in the water, children; wade in the water; Lord, don't you trouble the water."

_____

_____

_____

_____

_____

_____

_____

_____

DAY 37

It Takes a Maude

Being Right or Being Effective? (Page 63)

HOW OFTEN DO YOU FIND YOURSELF "encouraging" your congregation to live out its mission statement? Where are the roadblocks? If the congregation moved forward on a particular ministry at your encouragement, how successful was it? Moreover, how long did the ministry last? What would this mission step look like if it came not from you but from a "Maude"?

As you offer this day of life and ministry to God, name your desire for "Maude" to come forward and find her/his voice within your church. Name a potential Maude in your prayer journal and begin to pray daily for this person.

_____

_____

_____

_____

_____

_____

DAY 38

It's Not About You

Reframe, not blame. (Page 103)

I BEGAN ATTEMPTING THIS PARADIGM SHIFT at a difficult point in my pastorate. Whispers outside my hearing were gaining voice. The church was headed into another repeat of the blame game. I chose to deal with a staff struggle using this new model. Rather than dealing with "he said/she said," I was intentional about keeping the bigger question before us: "What does this say about our church right now?"

One staff member resisted. Determined, she found power with a subculture, and the blame game progressed. Unfortunately, nobody wins that game, and the church now bears the scars of that pain.

Begin this morning practicing reframing issues of conflict and differences in your congregation. Reframe out loud and then offer your words to God in your prayer journal. After each naming issue pray these words:

"God, help us to break old habits that continue to wound your church. Help us not to get caught up in the pettiness of the moment but to reframe the issue. 'What does this say about our church right now?'"

_____

_____

_____

_____

_____

_____

DAY 39

Bad News/Good News

Who gives the bad news? (Page 64)

SOMETIMES WE GET LUCKY. Before reading *How to Get Along with Your Church*, I witnessed a major personnel issue showing its ugly face in my church. It was there long before I came, but I was where it would end. You know, the buck stops here. I felt totally responsible to handle this difficult situation. But, I am forever grateful to a key culture-bearer who stepped up and insisted on delivering the "bad news" himself. He had the right, like Esther. Thanks, Dan!

As you sit quietly this morning, think of difficult issues within your congregation. Is there an Esther or a Dan you can trust to deliver the bad news? Can you honor and empower the key culture-bearer in this way? Pray for God's guidance in letting go.

Let your morning prayer be sung or spoken with the words of this African American spiritual:

I'm gonna live so God can use me anywhere Lord, anytime.

I'm gonna live so God can use me, anywhere Lord, anytime.

DAY 40

Running on Empty

Zero balance in the culture bank! (Page 93)

THE PASTOR WHO CUT DOWN THE Wesley tree had zero balance in cultural capital. His action destroyed a symbol of the church's culture, though he had absolutely no clue of its value. None of us wants to run such a risk. So, today it is time for you to look at your own cultural capital account.

Who are the key culture-bearers in your congregation?

What have you invested in the last forty days to gain cultural capital?

As you offer this day to God, sit quietly and think about your culture bank.

Begin to write in your journal the first name of three key culture-bearers. Next to each name write what you have done to gain their trust. Below this list, journal three things you will do to build up your cultural capital.

Begin your spoken prayer, naming each of these persons. As you sit with God, see their faces. Look for the goodness of God in each of them. Contemplate on how their cultural capital can help you and your congregation.

_____

_____

_____

_____

_____

_____

DAY 41

Still Looking Beneath the Surface

Levels of culture (Page 6)

The wise leader is like water. Water cleanses and refreshes all creatures; water freely and fearlessly goes deep beneath the surface of things; water is fluid and responsive…like water, the leader is yielding…. Because the leader does not push, the group does not resent or resist.[10]

As you prepare for this day of learning, take time to think of ways that biblical text uses water as a metaphor for life. What happens when water is scarce? What happens when water rages and floods? Journal your thoughts as a prayer from the wise leader you are becoming. Be attentive to the ways your leadership can cleanse and refresh, as well as the ways your leadership can push and destroy. Close your prayer with thanksgiving to God for the gift of life-giving water.

_____

_____

_____

_____

_____

OOO

DAY 42

Space to Be

Handling conflict (Page 108)

AS YOU CONTINUE TO LEARN MORE ABOUT your church's culture, you may
be surprised at how difficult it is to "be" in the midst of this transforming
work. All of us have difficulty living in the in-between times of waiting.
This is one of my personal experiences in the midst of transition.

On one most difficult day shortly after the death of my father, filled with
anxiety, I walked out onto the back porch. On the corner of the wall was
an ugly green blob. My eyes could not leave it. As I stood there in my
trance, someone came out the door. Seeing this thing, he knocked it
down and stomped it. Tears from nowhere streamed down my cheeks as I
reached down to pick up the butterfly in process. So strange was its
changing appearance it was crushed, even unto death. Fear struck me, for
what was going on inside and outside of this gentle creature was so fright-

ening to others that it would not be allowed to continue to transform. In the "waiting," it was destroyed because it was not what others expected it to be.[11]

Give yourself space to "be" this morning. Close your eyes and imagine that you are being held in this cocoon by God, as you learn in order to be part of the transforming grace God is offering to you and to your church. In your prayer journal write your feelings and your struggles of living in this "waiting."

_____

_____

_____

_____

_____

_____

_____

OOO

DAY 43

And If I Decide, What Then?

How do you know? (Page 113)

DURING MY DOCTORAL STUDIES, one of the books I found meaningful to transitions groups that I facilitated was Trina Paulus's *Hope for the Flowers*. It is a childlike story that many of us adults would do well to read over and over again. It is about two caterpillars who have to make a choice. They can choose to remain in their comfortable skin or to take a major risk to fully become the beautiful creatures God created them to be. Yellow is the first to make her decision, and her questions are ours as well:

"How does one become a butterfly?. . . You must want to fly so much that you are willing to give up being a caterpillar. You mean to die? . . . yes and no . . . what looks like you will die but what is really you will live . . . . And if I decide to become a butterfly, . . . what do I do?"[12]

This morning you have created time and sacred space to take a long, loving look at your decision to change. As you offer your prayer to God in your journal, answer the questions Yellow asks first about your pastorate. Then answer those questions for your congregation. Open yourself to the images of cocooning and transformation. Share this image with two persons today.

_____

_____

_____

_____

_____

⊙●⊙

DAY 44

I Never Saw It Coming!

Conflict around pastors can also emerge when the pastor takes a calculated risk. (Page 95)

WE CLERGY HAVE OUR CAUSES. We want our churches to step up and be who they say they are. We "hear" what they say they want—to bring in more children, to be warm and friendly.... But, when we find ways to make that happen, POW!!! We are ambushed. Sometimes the wounds are mere scratches, but more often they are deep, leaving scars that never heal. And these words are the cries of God's servants: "I never saw it coming."

As you prepare to chat with God today, begin by taking a long look at your present ministry.

What is it you are doing?

Where is the resistance?

What assumptions are at stake?

Have you been ambushed, too?

As you think on these things, offer them to God in your journal prayer.

It is not easy being a minister of God, but we surely are in the best of company.

Over and over again the Psalmist was ambushed:

Let the words from the 56th Psalm remind you of our commonality, and of God's faithfulness.

_____

_____

_____

_____

_____

_____

_____

DAY 45

Am I a Wisdom Seeker?

A learning spirit (Page 77)

FOR OVER FORTY DAYS YOU HAVE BEEN SEEKING wisdom about the culture of your congregation. You have learned much about them and you are learning some important things about yourself. Guiding your church to learn how to name its shared assumptions and how to develop new shared assumptions that will replace those that no longer work takes time and a learning spirit. You are on your way!

Be contemplative this morning. Take a long, loving look at the real. Look at what you have learned thus far and what you want to learn. Offer your wisdom to God for blessing.

_____

_____

_____

_____

_____

_____

_____

DAY 46

Are We Up to the Challenge?

Busyness, Vision, and Ministry (Page 56)

IF A VISION CONSISTS OF A PARTICULAR SET of espoused values, the pastor's challenge is to help the congregation put this set of values to the test. In order to create new assumptions and discover the ways in which old assumptions need altering, the congregation applies the values named by the vision to all the decisions that they make.

Once more, the prophetic words of a little-known prophet, Habukkuk, speak clearly to the leaders of churches today. This is a word we should hold in our memory, Habukkak 2:2.

Before you journal your prayer to God this morning, re-read this text and sit with it. Remember that you cannot write your church's vision, but you can lead them to discern and then live it. You are learning much about the purpose of your leadership. Take time to write three ways in which you can lead your church in testing its old assumptions while keeping its vision in front of them.

_____

_____

_____

_____

_____

_____

_____

DAY 47

Fear Not!!!

God is with us. (Page 110)

BY NOW YOU MAY BE FACING some honest fears. You are not alone. Throughout the biblical story the faithful of God have been reminded over and over again:

FEAR NOT.

This day as you open to God, offer, as your *gift,* your fears, as a gift
Name them.
Write them.
Gift them to God.

As you pray:

> Sustaining One, I am frightened.
> Fear not.
> Darkness overcomes me, yet I find no rest.
> Fear not
> They twist my words.
> Fear not.
> I have no voice.
> Fear not.
> Sustaining One, accept my fears as honest offerings and transform them
> into faith.

_____

_____

_____

_____

_____

_____

DAY 48

Deep and Wide

Cultural Symbolism (Page 97)

SEVERAL YEARS AGO I WAS CALLED AS the first full-time pastor of a beautiful historic church. My name was "permanently" attached to their sign so that all who passed by would see that finally their pastor had arrived. They spent time, money, and energy on decorating my office with custom furnishings. Everything had to look good!

The manse was nearby, so in the evenings often I would drop by my office, inevitably turning off lights as I headed home. To my surprise, every morning those lights would be back on. Eventually a member spoke to me and asked me to leave the lights on, even at night. It wasn't that he didn't want me working there at night—just leave those lights on. "We want the community to know our pastor is here." The light was an important symbol of pastoral presence to the congregation and to the community.

As you begin this day, pray the words of this little phrase we have taught the children for many years. Share with God in your journal prayer the symbols you have discovered in the culture of your congregation…as you continue to discover how deep and wide their symbols go:

Deep and wide, deep and wide, there's a fountain flowing deep and wide.
Deep and wide, deep and wide, there's a fountain flowing deep and wide.
Amen.

_____

_____

_____

_____

_____

_____

_____

_____

○○○

DAY 49

"You Gotta Serve Somebody"

How will we live together? (Page 106)

EVERY NOW AND THEN WHEN I am working on a sermon, a song pops into my head and I just can't let it go. It is true. Bob Dylan had the theology right—we all serve somebody.

That song came into my head along with the text from Joshua 24 several years ago, and it found its way back into my head as I find myself praying for and with you today. The lyrical and the biblical texts are texts for both pastors and churches. They are reminders about making the choice that matters most. The words retell the story of God's people. It is a story of remembering, and a story of knowing whose we are.

This morning as you prepare to serve God, read the words of Joshua. Remember the faithfulness of God to people like us. Give thanks to God as you journal your prayer, remembering God's faithfulness and your response to choose to serve God. Now, prepare to ask the question to your congregation: Whom will we serve?

_____

_____

_____

_____

_____

_____

_____

_____

DAY 50

Surrender to the Silence

Know thyself. (Page 118)

IF THINGS ARE GOING GREAT FOR YOU TODAY, will you bear with the rest of us whose days are less than good? Some time ago, during a spiritual breakdown in my own life, I began to fear that God had given up on me. I had left a congregation that I loved, a call I deeply believed in, all because of the power of a determined subculture. I ached for months. Maybe you can relate, as I do, to these words. Renita Weems writes:

I had been seduced out into the water where God knew I could not
swim,
  and left there to flail and figure out for myself how not to drown.
After what felt like years of flailing about, when I saw that (for reasons
I still
haven't been able to fathom) I wasn't going to drown, I began to calm
down and
stop fighting the waters.[13]

I continued my protest to God but, finally, I began to accept God's
silence as a place of recreating my pastoral identity.

This morning, imagine you are sitting encircled by clergy who have
cried out to God, only to hear nothing at all. Envision their faces, their
posture, their emptiness as you slowly read the prayer from Psalm 43. If
you are "one of us," journal your prayer as you begin to pay attention to
the silent voice of the Spirit around you.

_____

_____

_____

_____

_____

_____

DAY 51

The Unspeakable "C"

Going against the grain (Page 110)

CONFLICT HAPPENS—especially in the church. If we can learn how to see the deeper cultural factors at work, the church actually can be countercultural in our ways of working through conflict. This morning we will slowly pray Paul's hymn to the church in Philippi, as found in Philippians 2:1–14.

Sit with these words.

Pay attention to what is stirring in you

Offer those stirrings to God in your journal prayer.

Before you leave this space, slowly re-read the text in silence.

_____

_____

_____

_____

_____

_____

_____

DAY 52

Marginality

Being on the edge (Pages 79, 108)

IT IS CONFESSION TIME: I get too involved in the life of my church! Before learning this new model, I stood on edges everywhere, but when I am serving a church, I get right in the center of everything!

As I think more about it, in the rest of my living, I have always lived on the edge.

So, naturally, I find the labyrinth a meaningful prayer tool. However, you won't find me sitting for long periods of time at the meaningful center of any labyrinth. Rather, I'm the one intentionally putting my toes over the lines—walking on the edges.

I have learned the hard way that marginality is an important tool that empowers a pastor to stand on the edge of a congregation's life, in order to lead, guide, and support its vision.

As your journal prayer today, sit for a while asking yourself, "Where am I standing with my congregation?"

Draw a circle and mark its center with a cross to represent your church.

Locate yourself on this circle with an asterisk*.

Ask God to move with you to the margin.

As you conclude your prayer time, mark where you are moving with a carat (>).

_____

_____

_____

_____

_____

OOO

DAY 53

Tired, Empty and Never Enough

Every church has to have a reason to exist. (Page 85)

ARE THESE FAMILIAR PHRASES within your congregation?:

"We are tired, worn out. We can't do everything."

"We are just a little church. Our resources are limited."

As you sit in this sacred space, open your Bible to Mark 6:30–44, the story of Jesus' feeding of more than five thousand people. Remember, the task at hand seemed overwhelming. The disciples, though perplexed and tired, still did what Jesus asked. When the response was made, there was more than enough for everyone.

As you invite God to sit awhile with you, begin to imagine what your church might look like if one of your congregation's submerged beliefs was "there is always enough for others." As you journal your prayers, begin to form the question for your church.

For example, do we really believe God is faithful? Do we believe that if God calls us to feed the hungry in our community, we will be abundantly filled? Sit with the questions you form today and carry them with you throughout the day. Ask one of the questions to a member of your congregation as you continue to pray for sacred abundance.

_____

_____

_____

_____

_____

_____

_____

DAY 54

Navigating the Waters

Uncovering Assumptions (Pages 54, 55)

As you continue to discover some of what is in the mud of the swamp —those basic, shared assumptions that are part of your church's culture— you will have to learn how to navigate the waters between those that are helpful and those that could be damaging to their potential for vitality. If you are tackling some of the assumptions head on, you may be headed for impasse. You will be more helpful to your congregation by increasing your cultural capital by finding ways to bring deserved recognition to the persons and values represented by the assumption. From that point, you will be in a stronger position to respond and model an eventual modification of this assumption.

As you prepare to navigate today, offer to God the assumptions that make you uneasy and seem to block the passages to vitality in your church. List three. Then list three ways in which you can honor the person or persons who hold deeply to these values. Pray for them by name as you continue to seek the Spirit's guidance in learning how to get along with your church.

_____

_____

_____

_____

_____

_____

_____

○●○

DAY 55

Learning to Let Go

Busyness, Vision, and Ministry (Page 56)

WHAT IF THE REAL MIRACLE OF THE LOAVES and fishes looks less like abundance and more like trusting, sharing, and risking letting go? Megan McKennan reminds us that, not unlike today, women with children did not head out for the day without carrying enough food for their children. What if the real miracle of the loaves and fishes has little to do with those fed and everything to do with those who trusted Jesus? Though they, too, were tired and hungry, they risked letting go and shared what they had.[14]

As you pray through this text, note in your journal ways your congregation could hear this story. How can you open them to share their stories of faith? Can you imagine creating a sacred space for taking such a risk?

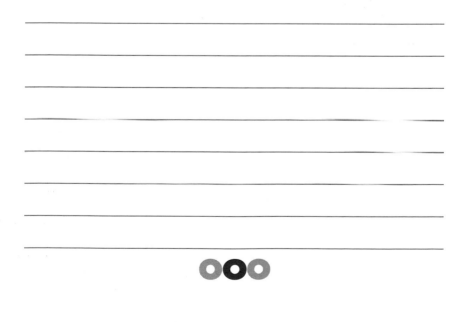

DAY 56

Can These Bones Live?

A declining church culture is rigid: It appears to be strong, but is actually brittle. (Page 107)

By now you may be wondering, "Can these bones live?" If your congregation is like the majority of congregations throughout the U.S., it is in decline. But, decline is not numerical. Congregations in decline are rigid, holding tightly to what used to work and not interested in the streams of culture around them.

This morning sit with God and put on your visual walking shoes. You are headed into another valley of dry, brittle bones with a fellow prophet named Ezekiel (Ex. 37).

First, read these verses slowly out loud. Listen for a word or phrase that startles (or disgusts) you. After a time of silence, read the text again to yourself, paying attention to the word that has stirred something in you. Rest in the valley. Then offer to God what you have heard and seen in this valley that can offer new life to your congregation.

_____

_____

_____

_____

_____

_____

_____

_____

DAY 57

Keep on Reading the Road Map

This four-function model gives a basic road map for moving your church forward. (Page 83)

I HAVE NO PROBLEM STOPPING TO ASK directions—but I want directions that are going to take me where I want to go, and I have to be able to use them. The "what, who, how, and why" help pastors like you and me find the way to lead our churches toward vitality. Sometimes we are so certain we know the way that we forget to look where we're going, much less ask for directions. Keep on reading that road map!

As you offer your journey to God today, sketch your road map. What does your church do? Who does your congregation treat as "one of us"? Who makes the decisions?

Why does your church exist? Where does your energy need to be to help your congregation keep the "why, who, what, and how" up front? How are you going to find your way?

_____

_____

_____

_____

_____

_____

_____

DAY 58

Let's Just Stay Up Here!

The evolution of your congregation's culture (Page 66)

I CAN JUST IMAGINe MYSELF on top of the mountain with Jesus. Like Peter, I'd be ready to build just about anything to be able to stay on top. Wouldn't you? So, we can't blame churches for wanting to do the same. No matter where our church locates itself on the life cycle, it has work to do to remain a vital witness. None of us can sit on the mountaintop and look around. We all have to come back to the work of ministry.

As you prepare for seeking God today, read Matthew's story of the Transfiguration of Jesus (Matthew 17: 6.) Read it again and wonder: Where is your church in this story? Would they feel left behind when Jesus heads up the mountain?

If someone from your church were to go to the mountaintop, who would it be? Can you envision helping your church understand its need to be flexible in order to sustain or gain vitality? Share your thoughts as prayer in your journal, asking God to transfigure your congregation as you seek to be a vital Christian witness in your community.

DAY 59

Keep Watch!

Vision=Hope (Page 75)

THE PROPHETIC VOICE OF Habakkuk is rarely heard in our churches. We are so ready to plan programs, lead committee meetings, and try to find ways to increase our finances that we forget what we need to look out for. Habakkuk did not forget. He waited. Yahweh's word to him is the word we need to share with our congregations.

As you journal your prayer of hopes, fears, frustrations, and thanksgivings, sit with the first three verses of Habakkuk 2. What do you hear? Is your church keeping watch? What might that look like? Have you written your vision? Is it clear? It is important to note that sometimes we need to wait. What might your church do in the waiting? Offer your thoughts to God in your journal prayer as you continue to watch, wait, and see God's purpose for your church.

_____

_____

_____

_____

_____

$\bullet\circ\bullet$

DAY 60

What's Happening Here?

Pastors who are leaders (Page 82)

SOMETIMES WE PASTORS WORK REALLY hard to make something happen,
only to find that as soon as we turn our heads, or head out the door, things
go back to the way they've always been done. For me, it is celebrating
communion by intinction. Jesus did not have little cups and wafers. He
sat around a table with his beloved friends, blessed and broke some bread,
passed it around, and then they dipped a piece of that bread into a cup.
Sharing the sacrament by breaking bread and dipping it into a cup is the-
ologically sound, but for many Christians, it is an unwelcome change.
And, as soon as I am out of the picture, back come the little cups. What's
happening here?

Pastors who are leaders need to take seriously the idea that simply talking about something new does not make it happen.

Sit for a moment as you gather your thoughts about the changes you
have made or are making in your church. Knowing what you have learned,

name a change that you have talked about that has not happened. How are you involving key culture-bearers in this change? What does the resistance look and sound like? How might you invite others into this new possibility? Journal your thoughts as prayer to our ever-creating God.

_____

_____

_____

_____

_____

_____

_____

_____

DAY 61

If You Can Keep Your Head!

A Ministry of Presence (Page 56)

YOU ARE CHANGING, LEARNING, GROWING. As your congregation discovers both the helpful and harmful shared assumptions, anxiety may increase. Know that every attempt will be made to pull you into the center of their fears. Be fully present, but stay on the margin.

As you begin this day, begin by praying some of the words of Rudyard

Kipling's "If": "If you can keep your head, when all about you are losing theirs and blaming you...."

In your prayer journal, write these words and complete this sentence with:

Your hopes for your church:

_____

_____

_____

Your frustrations with your church:

_____

_____

_____

Your plans for your church:

_____

_____

_____

DAY 62

Stagnant Waters and New Streams

Cultural confluence (Page 20)

THERE ARE THOSE IN YOUR congregation who are ready for things to "settle down." But, you are learning that change takes time and intentional study of the culture of a congregation. Each time you find yourself pushed into a corner by an anxious member, take a deep breath and feel the renewing presence of the Spirit.

Remember, the culture of your church is always changing. If the streams stop flowing, your water becomes stagnant, and nothing can live there.

In your time with God, close your eyes and see a flowing stream. Notice the sound it makes. Notice its color. Notice the life in and around it. Try to see what it flows into and what that body of water looks like.

Offer your church's stream to God, and pray for new streams to fill and refill it, as you pray these words:

Spiritus, blow where you will and not where we expect or desire.
Spiritus, giver of life, disturb our stagnant waters. Swirl us into
unknown streams and raise us up over the rapids, even as you continue to
fill us with grace, peace, joy and love that breathes life.
Amen.

_____

_____

_____

_____

_____

_____

_____

_____

OOO

DAY 63

Damming Up the Streams

Espoused Values and Uncovering Assumptions (Page 54)

HOW MANY TIMES HAVE YOU HEARD THEM SAY IT: "We are a warm and friendly church"? So, why is it the newcomers have such a difficult time finding their place here? Why do folks visit a few times and never join us?

This morning, meditate more about the streams of culture that could be flowing into your church. Could deeply-held assumptions be damming up the streams?

Share your thoughts with God in your journal today.

What water is there stays for a while and then it evaporates. Notice that no new water can come into the stream. Life in and around the stream begins to die. How long do you think it might take until the stream becomes stagnant? What will it look like then? How will it smell? How can you help your church break the dam?

_____

_____

_____

_____

_____

_____

_____

_____

DAY 64

Asking the Hard Questions, Again

Final words (Page 130)

FOR AT LEAST TWO MONTHS YOU HAVE BEEN ASKING hard questions. As you ponder those learnings today, it is time to begin to ask an even more difficult question: *How can I make a difference here?*

In your prayer offering, sit with that question. After a time of silent reflection, offer it to God. Continue to stay with the question as you note in your journal what you hear. Continue to listen for God in the voices of those around you in days to come.

_____

_____

_____

_____

_____

_____

_____

_____

DAY 65

What If I Have to Go?

When to say goodbye. (Page 114)

THE TIME COMES WHEN EACH OF US has a disappointment in our ministries. Sometimes the call doesn't happen, the opportunity never knocks. Other times what looked like the right church doesn't turn out that way.

Parker Palmer offers us another way of looking at these situations:

As often happens on the spiritual journey, we have arrived at the heart of a paradox: each time a door closes, the rest of the world opens up. All we need to do is stop pounding on the door that just closed; turn around—which puts the door behind us—and welcome the largeness of life that now lies open to our souls. That door that closed kept us from entering a room, but what now lies before us is the rest of reality.[15]

Wherever you find yourself in your pastoral vocation, as you choose this time to sit with God today, look at where you are. Ask God to help you turn around and move into whatever lies before you with faith and grace.

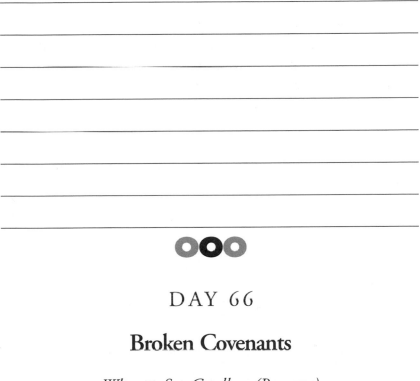

DAY 66

Broken Covenants

When to Say Goodbye. (Page 114)

IT MAY OR MAY NOT BE TIME FOR you to move on. Biblical stories remind us that servants of God do just that: they move on. Still, transitions are not easy. You have learned much about this congregation that will help you transition to being a better pastor, whether you stay or move on. Still, broken covenants bring deep pain to clergy who have faithfully sought to serve God. Often, the wounds are deep, and they cause us to question our sense of call itself.

When covenants are broken and no healing is offered, it is helpful to rediscover the Prayer of Examen, inviting God to look with us at every facet of our existence. We invite the Spirit to guide us as we scrutinize our deepest self, but also we ask that the life-giving light of Christ touch our brokenness and give genuine healing to our wounds. Today is the day to listen to this reminder:

> And even when we carry the burden of our inability to move a preoccupied people toward faithfulness, we must remember, there is indeed healing, redemption, and renewal available for those who seek to walk with God. That cure is offered in Christ through whom "we have redemption . . . according to the riches of his grace." (Ephesians 1:7)[16]

This day, ask God to guide you in the Prayer of Examen. Offer your wounds, your fears, and your love to the one who called you and calls you to healing even now.

DAY 67

Tapping into Forgotten Energy

Appreciative Inquiry (Page 83)

OFTEN WHEN WE STRUGGLE WITH HELPING churches rediscover God's purpose for them we find that the central focus is "what is wrong here." A colleague of ours, Mark Lau Branson, worked with such a church in decline, using the Appreciative Inquiry Process.

Appreciative Inquiry gives us a place to share stories of strengths and faithfulness as we learn more about the culture of our congregations.[17] Today, take time to look at your congregation in this way.

First, answer the questions for yourself. Second, arrange a time to gather a small group from within your congregation. Third, remind them that in learning more about the culture of the congregation, you have heard stories of strength and faithfulness. Fourth, read together Philippians 4:8.

Ask the group to pair off and ask each other the following questions. After a few minutes, gather the group. Share and bless the stories!

1. Remembering your entire experience at our church, when were you most excited and motivated? What made it exciting? How were you involved? Who else was involved? Describe how you felt.

---

2. What do you value most about our church? What is most important here to you? What do we do best?

_____

_____

_____

_____

_____

3. Make three wishes for the future of this church.

_____

_____

_____

_____

DAY 68

Remembering Your Call

Know thyself, again! (Page 118)

YESTERDAY YOU DID SOME REMEMBERING about your ministry with this particular church. As you continue to practice using the tools you are learning with *How to Get Along with Your Church,* it will be helpful to look at your call to ministry in a similar way.

As you sit with the following questions, take time to remember why you answered God's call, and offer your responses as your prayer in your journal.

1. As you look back on your service in ministry, when were you most alive, most fulfilled? Who were the people who were involved in that ministry with you?

_____

_____

_____

_____

_____

2. What were your hopes? Describe your feelings.

_____

_____

_____

_____

_____

3. What are the pieces of ministry that fill you with joy, or peace?

_____

_____

_____

_____

_____

4. What are three wishes that you hold for your ministry?

_____

_____

_____

_____

_____

_____

DAY 69

Still Searching!

Vision for a Church is…. (Page 57)

AFTER LOOKING AT YOUR CHURCH THROUGH a cultural lens, you may still be wondering what the church's vision should look like. Every member of your congregation has her or his own idea of what the church is to do. Now that you know everything must be measured against the vision, you may need a strong definition. Vision for a church is that distinctive picture of a possible future to which the congregation senses God is calling it.

As you and God sit quietly together, think on this definition of vision:

It speaks of the church's—distinctive—picture—possible future—
To which the CONGREGATION senses—GOD—calling it.
What would it look like if your church meditated on this thought for several Sundays?

O God, creator of possibility, speak to us. You have called us, yet we have difficulty hearing. We struggle so with living in the now, we cannot imagine the possibilities of tomorrow. Open our ears, our hearts, our minds, O Spirit. Be Thou our vision. Amen.

_____

_____

_____

_____

_____

_____

_____

DAY 70

Still Looking for that Vision

A Vision Consists of... (Page 77)

As your congregation begins to seek God's vision for their future, remember to look at what you are learning about artifacts, espoused and submerged values. A vision consists of a set of espoused values that are understood in some particular relationship with one another.

As you think more about your congregation's vision, make journal notes about the relatedness of espoused values to the deeply submerged values that are rarely, if ever, spoken out loud. In your prayer journal, connect them as best you can as you begin to get a picture of your church's vision today.

_____

_____

_____

_____

_____

_____

_____

DAY 71

Busyness or Ministry?

Making It Count. (Page 45)

PEOPLE WHO DON'T LIVE WITH CLERGY cannot understand why we "do so much." Sometimes that "doing" looks like busyness, but often it is the part of our ministry that matters most. I've found that sitting around the table eating pizza with youth is just as important a part of my ministry as leading a confirmation class. Heading out to a football game and sitting with members of my church whose son spends the game on the bench counts as ministry. Even sharing a cup of coffee with a member, who is troubled with all the changes going on in her church, is ministry.

As you prepare for this day of busyness, journal your prayer to God and name your plans and hopes to make the busyness of the day count as ministry. Can you imagine ways in which you might find time to spend with a member who is struggling with your questions?

Can you imagine being intentional today and checking in on someone who has been obviously absent in the last couple of months? As you think on these things, offer them to the One who will be present with you as well.

DAY 72

Even in Darkness

Land Mines (Page 8)

My experience of learning what really matters in my prayer journal always seems to involve times of darkness. During these times, I would seek the wisdom of my spiritual director. When she invited me to envision darkness as a womblike space from which all life comes, I began to embrace the darkness even as I searched for the light.

Today I invite you to claim the sacred space of darkness when it surrounds your ministry as you pray using the words of the psalmist in Psalm 139:7–18. Sit with these words. As you journal your prayer, offer God the darkness and light around you. Read the text again, and pay attention throughout the day to the word or phrase that captures or startles you.

_____

_____

_____

_____

○●○

DAY 73

Being Fully Present

Vision (Page 85)

REMEMBER THAT VISION PROVIDES ENERGY to perform, relate, and execute. As your church begins to seek its purpose (vision), be present with them. With wise use of your new tools, you can guide them in right paths.

As you meditate on a ministry of presence, guiding your church into a place of claiming its purpose, note in your prayer journal three ways you are being present to them. Remember, the task is not yours alone, and you are not alone in your ministry.

Take time to check in with one of the people you listed early in your journal as one you could count on for support. Let the words of this old spiritual dwell within you throughout the day:

> Guide my feet, while I run this race.
> Guide my feet, while I run this race.
> Guide my feet, while I run this race,
> Cause I don't want to run this race in vain.

_____

_____

_____

_____

_____

_____

_____

_____

DAY 74

How Can We Hear All the Voices?

Engage Church Members in the Process (Page 80)

When we are not in the room with you, it is simple to say, "You must engage church members in the process by listening to and working with their groups and activities."

But you and I know that a few loud, strong voices overpower and silence others who need to be heard. George and I have written an entire chapter about self and voicelessness in *Alligators in the Swamp: Power, Ministry, and Public Leadership*. But a friend of ours, Eric Law, offers a suggestion you can use today to provide a safe space for voices to be heard. He names it "mutual invitation."[18]

As you meditate this morning, imagine you are asking questions to members of your board. See their faces in your mind. Listen to the responses. Are there people who do not speak?

In your mind, experiment with the process of mutual invitation by explaining your desire to give all those present a safe space to voice their opinion. Present a situation or ask a question for the groups to discuss. Invite one person in each group to respond. No one in the group will interrupt or speak against the response. The person who begins will then invite another by name to respond, saying: "Mary, I invite you to respond." Mary may choose to respond or to pass. Either way, she will not contradict or criticize what has been said. All will be silent as she speaks or remains silent until she is ready to invite another by name to respond. This will continue until each person in the small group has had the opportunity to share their opinion. After each has had a turn, another turn is offered to anyone who passed before. Only after everyone has had an opportunity to speak can the group discuss what they have learned from one another.

This may first be done by using a biblical text if that helps your Board gain a level of comfort. As you imagine this, know that you will have to go from group to group with a reminder of the process. It is crucial that each be invited to respond by name and that no one interrupts or challenges another. In this way, a safe sacred space is created.

Offer your hopes to God in your prayer journal.

DAY 75

"Hey, Look at Us."

Assumptions and the life cycle (Page 104–6)

YOU MAY BE A PASTOR SERVING A CHURCH that is looking pretty good right now; your membership is proud of how their church is doing. Most of all, they like who they are and see no need to make any changes. At this stage on the life cycle, your church operates with several subcultures. Though they share some assumptions, each subculture has its own distinctive assumptions. Sorry, this is not your time as leader to rest!

The question you, as leader, must continue to ask is: "How will we live together?"

As you center yourself for this day, think of the ways in which the music department is competing with Christian Education. Is the adult Sunday school class holding onto its huge room while the nursery has outgrown its space? How do these subcultures view you? How will you claim your marginality, yet be fully present? Journal your thoughts as you offer them to the One who continues to lead and guide you in right pathways.

_____

_____

_____

_____

_____

_____

_____

DAY 76

How Can We Survive?

More assumptions about the life cycle (Page 106)

IS YOUR CHURCH LOSING MEMBERS, especially youth and children? Do new members leave within the first year? Do they say one thing, yet recoil when that one thing actually becomes reality? Welcome to the weakening church or the church in decline.

In most denominations, this stage of the life cycle represents the majority of our churches. Since fear of survival becomes the underlying motive, it is difficult for any pastor to survive at this church for long.

However, you have more tools than most pastors. You have been intentional about learning how to get along with your church in whatever stage you find it. You understand about fear, about subcultures, about artifacts, espoused values, and deeply held assumptions. You know the importance of earning cultural capital. You are making a difference, and your church can survive!

Sit quietly this morning and look closely at your church's culture. Journal your thoughts and offer them to God:

Who are the loud voices?
What is going on that challenges the old assumptions?
Where is the fear? Where is the resistance most clearly seen?
How can you maintain your marginality?
Can you reframe the question and ask: "What does this say about our church today?"

_____

_____

_____

_____

_____

_____

_____

_____

ooo

DAY 77

Is Your Church Ready For a New Thing?

. . . eyes fixed on a vision (Page 81)

THE PROPHETIC VOICE OF ISAIAH is never far from my heart or head. Like you, I want to see your church become the vital church God is calling it to be. But change is never easy.

Resistance to change is even greater in weakening churches. I have learned from this book that change has to come from within the congregation itself. So, perhaps the new thing is just to keep the question alive.

This morning re-read Isaiah 43:19–21. Find your congregation in the text. Can you imagine ways to invite them to wonder about what this new thing might be? In your journal, rewrite this text using your hopes for your congregation. How will they be best able to understand it? What would it mean to them to hear that the "new thing" God is offering will provide a way for them to offer praise?

_____

_____

_____

_____

_____

_____

_____

DAY 78

More Than Exhausted!

Biblical leave-taking (Page 115)

SOME DAYS WE PASTORS FIND OURSELVES EXHAUSTED. As those days pile up one after another, it becomes easier and easier to forget why we even try to do this thing called ministry.

While putting finishing touches on this companion for you, my husband and I spent some time with family in Oregon. If you've never experienced Oregon in late July, you must. It is green and sunny and the humidity is low. The tall trees provide natural air-conditioning for the farmhouse. All is restful, except for the computer and me.

Balanced against my great desire for a time of rest and renewal, Dad gave me the reminder God wanted me to hear, in the midst of my frustration with needing to get this book finished. As the tape began to play, I heard him sing the song he wrote years ago, sharing with his boys and me a clear picture of faith, and offering me another way to remember why we do what we do. He has graciously allowed me to share it with you (sorry you can't hear the guitar he played as he sang it):

Come, rest a while in the quiet of the morning. Clear, for a moment, all the pictures from your mind. If it helps, close your eyes. Now, think on this one thought:

Jesus Died; He Arose; Jesus Lives. We will die. We will Rise. We will live in Him.
Come, rest forever in the quiet of tomorrow.[19]

DAY 79

Necessary Tools

Cultures crossing (Page 92)

It's something we all know: we cannot get very far without the right tools, and some of us need more tools than others. This simple fact became crystal clear for my ministry when I read what George writes in another book for pastors about his Sears Craftsman toolbox. He describes his love of tinkering, as well as his desire to have just the right tool for the job.[20] That's what I thought seminary did for us: gave us all the right tools for the task of ministry. Wrong!!!

This morning, ask God to be with you as you list in your journal the new tools you are adding to your pastoral toolbox. How will these tools make a difference in your ministry? Can you envision sharing these tools with other pastors? With your own congregation? Do you realize that in using these tools, you are making a major paradigm shift that can help your congregation regain its vitality and purpose?

_____

_____

_____

_____

_____

_____

_____

DAY 80

Seeking God in the Midst of Transition

Voice of the Spirit (Page 134)

As a pastor and a "learner," you and your church are in a time of transition. You know that you are fully dependent on God in this liminal time of preparation, but, sometimes churchfolk want action—now! Be patient. Give yourself time to understand your church's culture, so that you can lead them. Only when you have helped your congregation understand its culture will your church be ready to experience the kind of lasting transformation that will lead to its vital witness.

As you prepare for the work of your ministry, sit for awhile and think about this time of learning as preparation for your church's transformation. In your prayer journal, list six things you have already learned about your church in the last forty plus days. Then note next to each listing what might have happened had you acted rather than taken the time to learn something first.

Offer your thoughts to God and let your prayer continue throughout the day, as you look for ways in which God is preparing you in the midst of this transition.

DAY 81

Check It Out!

Espoused values and triggered assumptions (Page 7)

ONE OF THE THINGS I have learned the hard way is that I make a lot of assumptions. In fact, we all make a lot of assumptions about each other and about the church. In order to be certain that the leaders of your church are on the same "track" as you are, check out your assumptions— often. Contemplative dialogue has been my guide for paying attention to how much I assume about others by using the ladder of inference.[21]

As you gather your thoughts and invite God to sit with you this morning, begin to check out some of the assumptions you are making. Here is an example to help you begin to think in this way:

> You walk down the hall and your boss walks by without speaking to you.
> At first you assume he didn't notice you; then you assume he ignored you.
> Maybe he didn't want to speak to you because he doesn't like or respect
> you. Or perhaps, you assume, he doesn't speak because he is about to fire
> you.

Note your thoughts in your prayer journal as you ask God to help you notice your assumptions today.

Practice checking out your assumptions in meetings and in conversations, saying something like: Let me see if I have this right, or—I assume you—or I just want to check in with you and see if I understand where you are coming from. . . .

_____

_____

_____

_____

_____

_____

_____

DAY 82

The One with the Most Marbles Always Wins?

Triggered assumptions (Page 100)

UNFORTUNATELY, WE KNOW THAT THE ONE with the most cultural capital in our churches has the most marbles, or power. What most of us don't know, or want to talk about, is that we all have power in the church. That in itself is not a bad thing. Without power we cannot lead. But misuse of power is destructive. *Alligators in the Swamp* is a book about power and ministry that will add another important tool to your toolbox.[22]

Today it is time to begin to think about how you see power being used in your church.

Who are the people who have the most power?

_____

_____

_____

How is that power used?

_____

_____

_____

Who are the powerless ones?

_____

_____

_____

How involved are they in the decision-making process of your church?

_____

_____

_____

What does your power look like?

_____

_____

_____

Are you willing to share power?

_____

_____

_____

Offer these thoughts to God as you write them today.

_____

_____

_____

Sit for a while and think of the ways Jesus used power.

○●○

DAY 83

It's Not About You!

Reframe, not blame (Page 103)

Most pastors carry deep inside stories of struggle and pain. Few of us are willing to talk much about them because we have been made to believe that they're entirely our fault. You have learned to "reframe" what is going on in your church when conflict arises. Now you need to learn to reframe the conflicts that cause you pain. Churches in the weak or decline stages of the life cycle need a scapegoat. Remember, it is not about you, but all about what is going on with the church.

This is important space for you and God. Today invite God to sit with you as you journal your thoughts about a painful experience in a church you serve(d). Describe how you are feeling as you think about this situation. What was going on with the culture and subcultures of that church?

Ask the question you have learned to ask your own congregation whenever conflict arises: What does this say about our church right now? Offer your thoughts as prayer to God and remember, it's not about you.

_____

_____

_____

_____

_____

_____

DAY 84

No Cultural Divide!

Cultural capital (Page 21)

TWO DAYS AFTER WE WERE MARRIED, George and I headed off to Kenya, where he would teach several classes at the Presbyterian College in Kikuyu. The classroom was filled with nearly fifty bright seminarians from tribes throughout East Africa. Imagine our delight when one of the five women in the class gave this response to George's question regarding shared assumptions: "The church where I did my internship is nearby. The women are in charge. They say they are warm and friendly, but really, they have all the answers and they want everything their way."

Those students "got it." The discussion was lively, and we learned much from them. There is no cultural divide in learning about a church's culture.

As you journal today, think of the things you hear about other churches. Then begin to look at those things through your cultural-learning lens. Being able to see what is really going on in other churches will help you see through the clutter at your church.

Offer your thoughts to God this morning as you give thanks for our sisters and brothers serving churches throughout the world.

_____

_____

_____

_____

_____

_____

_____

_____

_____

○●○

DAY 85

Please, No Snakes!

Wise as serpents, and innocent as doves (Page 135)

IN OUR TRAINING AND COACHING WITH CHURCHES, George has one text that is his alone to share. When he preached in the college in Kenya, the students shouted their "amens" and beat the drums as he spoke of it. Personally, I had difficulty reading it aloud for that service of worship. The text is Matthew's story of Jesus' sending out the twelve. I admit to you that I have been most grateful for Jesus' words in parts of this text, especially in verse 14: "Shake the dust off your feet as you leave." But I confess, I quit reading there.

Surely Jesus wouldn't ask us to be "wise as serpents and innocent as doves."

But, Jesus did say just that. You are becoming wise. Your wisdom has increased and will continue to grow because you are choosing to be a learner. (Still, let's keep the snake thing to ourselves!)

Read Matthew 10:1–16. Jesus was clearly preparing his disciples and us for the ministries to which we are called. We do have to be wise in order to live out our calling.

As you offer your prayer to God this morning, in your journal note how you are using your new wisdom to get along with your church. Does your innocence look different than before?

_____

_____

_____

_____

_____

_____

_____

DAY 86

How Will You Say It?

Conflict puts culture to the test (Page 96)

IT'S ONLY NATURAL FOR US TO THROW UP our hands when conflict rears its not-so-pretty head again! However, if we keep framing the situations we face in psychological or theological terms, we will not be able to tap into the cultural energy at work in our churches. Every time you get a whiff of conflict, be careful of the question you ask.

Let God be your partner this morning as you think about how you choose to respond to conflict in your church. You have practiced this earlier, but in order to be prepared to lead your church through conflict, you will want to practice this internally and daily. So today, partner with God as you offer your journal prayer. Mark this page and read it often: WHAT DOES THIS SAY ABOUT OUR CHURCH RIGHT NOW?

As you ponder that question, you will begin to have new insight into the conflict. Remember a recent conflict. In your journal, see if you can relate in this way:

Circumstance of the conflict: artifacts

Discourse: espoused values

Opposition or uncertainty: shared assumptions that are still covered

Offer your thoughts in your journal to the One who partners in ministry with you, Emmanuel, God with us.

_____

_____

_____

_____

_____

_____

_____

DAY 87

What Will You Do?

Making it count (Page 53)

CARLA IS A REGISTERED NURSE WITH TWO YOUNG CHILDREN. Some of the older women in your church have invited Carla to join them for Bible study and lunch each month. Carla works nights and is excited about being able to get to know these women, who seem to know so much about the Bible. She comes twice, but the next month she doesn't show up. Two women check on her, and she tells them she had to work that day. You notice Carla has not been in worship for several weeks. What will you do, now that you have some idea of the culture of your church?

As you think about this situation, journal your thoughts, your frustrations and make some assumptions of what could be going on with Carla.

List in your journal the artifacts she could have noticed in your church, the things that she heard people say (espoused values). What shared assumptions could be affecting this situation?

Pray for your church and for all the Carlas we turn away.

_____

_____

_____

_____

_____

_____

_____

DAY 88

Keep Telling the Stories

Tips for adoption (Page 35)

SOMETIMES I WONDER HOW MY RURAL CHURCH ever put up with me. I can still remember Oktoberfest: hot dogs and marshmallows roasted on wire coat-hangers; children running wild around an open campfire; and me complaining like crazy about the germs they were being exposed to as their wide-open mouths reached to bob for apples in a tub of water. I was so busy looking at what felt wrong to me that I couldn't celebrate that this little church was filled with life for a night, just like the old-timers remembered it. And that was what mattered! It's hard to be adopted when you don't take time to celebrate where people are.

As you sit quietly today, think of the stories you have heard and missed in your church. How can you begin to bring those stories to life again? Offer as your journal prayer these stories and your plan to celebrate the oral culture of your church.

_____

_____

_____

_____

_____

_____

_____

DAY 89

Words That Keep Me Awake at Night!

Being Right or Being Effective (Page 109)

LAST YEAR GEORGE AND I attended our denomination's yearly meeting. We were invited to be guests at a breakfast sponsored by the redevelopment committee where *How To Get Along with Your Church* was recommended as a resource to churches. After breakfast, we were greeted by a woman who was serving her first call as the pastor of a small rural church. She expressed her frustration that her church just didn't get it; they didn't understand what they needed to do, and she was "determined" to change them. Her intentions were good, but you know she was headed for big trouble. We offered to meet with her, but she was off to the next gathering. For the sake of her ministry, I hope she read the book.

Sit for a moment as you begin to think of the ways you have tried to change your church. What words would you offer this sister in Christ? How can you begin to share your new wisdom with other pastors? Offer your thoughts as prayer in your journal as you seek the Spirit's guidance in helping others.

_____

_____

_____

_____

_____

_____

_____

_____

_____

●○●

DAY 90

This is the Day the Lord Has Made

Remember God is with us (Page 110)

A faithful elder in my former congregation was always there to remind me: *This is the day the Lord has made; we will rejoice and be glad in it.* Some of those days were filled with joy, others with bitter tears. But Stewart was right, they were each and all days created by God. And that is more than enough to fill us with deep joy.

As you worship God this morning, give thanks for the day, and for the Stewarts who remind us to be glad.

_____

_____

_____

_____

_____

_____

_____

_____

DAY 91

How Can I Get Them on Board?

A commitment to member involvement (Page 78)

You've been working hard to get a handle on the culture of your congregation. But you may be experiencing the frustration of being the only one who will pay attention. You know you cannot change your church's culture, but you also see that change needs to happen. What is your plan?

In your prayer journal, write a short plan for how to involve others in learning more about your church. What have your tried thus far? Who has responded? Where is the resistance? What would this look like if you noted it using artifacts, espoused values, and shared assumptions? Are key culture-bearers involved? How will you involve them so that they can reach out to others? Offer your thoughts as prayer to God.

_____

_____

_____

_____

_____

_____

_____

_____

○●○

DAY 92

Midwife or CEO?

The pastor's role is…to "midwife" the parish's own decision.
(Page 97)

I CAN STILL NAME THE TIMES I have tried to help a congregation move in new pathways. Sometimes it worked . . . for a while. Other times, my efforts fell flat and I found myself exhausted and empty. We are called to be midwives, not CEOs.

As you sit with God this morning, remember the work of midwives. In your prayer journal, list the ways you can imagine your pastorate using the midwife metaphor.

Now list the ways you recognize God being the loving midwife with and for your ministry.

_____

_____

_____

_____

_____

_____

_____

_____

OOO

DAY 93

Who Pastors the Pastor?

Know thyself. (Page 118)

JOE IS A GOOD PASTOR. He is at every meeting; you see him at community gatherings. His smile warms you. He's one lucky guy. His church looks great. His wife does a great job with his two small sons. She never complains about his long hours. They are just one beautiful family. Or are they?

Who pastors the pastor?

As you think about Joe this morning, be honest about all the things you hide inside, too.

Where do you take your frustration and sorrow?

How do you make time for your family?

Are you making time to meet with those persons you named as support for you?

Is it time to find additional support for you and your family?

Where will you turn for that support?

_____

_____

_____

_____

_____

_____

_____

_____

○●○

DAY 94

What About Mary?

Make it count (Page 53)

SUPPOSE YOU HAVE DECIDED it is time for you to go, or perhaps it is the time you will be reassigned. What will you do about Mary? Mary came to your church six months ago. She is a single mother with three children. After her first Sunday, she came to you asking for financial help, and you did what you could. Since then Mary has done odd jobs around the church, but nobody knows her desperate financial state. Mary is a hard worker and a proud woman.

Her boys would be embarrassed if anyone knew they live in a one-room apartment with whatever food they can get from the food pantry. Now you are leaving. Your church members say they want to reach out to others, but you know better.

What will you do about Mary?

Maybe there has been a Mary in your ministry. If not, there could be. This morning, practice your "learnings" and journal your response to Mary's situation. Offer your prayers for the Marys around us and for the churches that she enters.

_____

_____

_____

_____

_____

_____

_____

DAY 95

Take Your Time

I thought I knew (Page 1)

Churches call pastors for a purpose. We pastors answer calls because we believe we can make a difference. We pray about our calls, and the churches pray for the right pastor to lead their church. But remember what you are learning, and take your time.

If you are not appointed to a church, but have a choice in the process, look carefully and ask questions that may help you see deeper into the swamp of the church.

Most of us cannot really begin to know our congregations until we have been there for a few months. Here are a few tips to remember during that time: As you learn about the culture of your church, be present with them. Accept them where they are. Do not change anything. Earn cultural capital. Get adopted!

Sit for a few moments as you reconsider these words. Then note in your prayer journal ways in which you are seeking adoption by your church—no matter how long you have been there. Offer your notes as prayer.

_____

_____

_____

_____

_____

_____

DAY 96

Keep Listening for That Call

I LOVE THE SLOGAN THE United Church of Christ is using right now: "God is still speaking." Could it be that God is still also calling?

As you journal your prayer this morning, list some ways you are hearing God's call to you and to your church.

_____

_____

_____

_____

_____

_____

_____

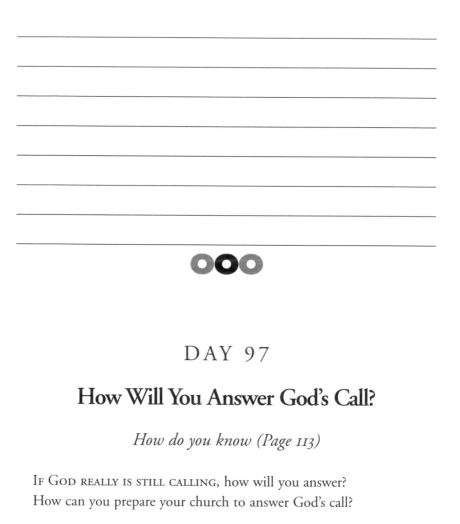

DAY 97

How Will You Answer God's Call?

How do you know (Page 113)

IF GOD REALLY IS STILL CALLING, how will you answer?
How can you prepare your church to answer God's call?

This morning as you ponder the answers to these questions, may your response and the response of your church be found in the words to this amazing hymn. Share it with them on Sunday. The refrain is:

Here I am Lord, is it I Lord?
I have heard you calling in the night.
I will go, Lord, if you lead me.
I will hold your people in my heart.

_____

_____

_____

_____

_____

_____

_____

DAY 98

Grace Abounds!

Know thyself —really! (Page 118)

BY NOW YOU MAY BE THINKING A LOT about the mistakes you've made in your ministry. "If only I'd known" rears its ugly head far too often in my own life. I sure see my mistakes more clearly after learning more about

How to Get Along with Your Church. But, grace abounds, even for pastors, and we don't need to be so hard on ourselves.

Thank goodness, grace appears to us when we least expect it. A couple of years ago, in the midst of my own "learning," I was so deeply moved while reading a piece from the prologue of Rick Bragg's *All Over But the Shoutin'* that I used it as a call to confession one Sunday. I share it as a grace note for you today:

> I watched one of the birds attack its own reflection in the side mirror of a truck. It hurled its body again and again against that unyielding image, until it pecked a crack in the glass, until the whole mirror was smeared with blood. It was as if the bird hated what it saw there, and discovered all too late that all it was seeing was itself. I asked an old man who worked for my uncle Ed . . . why he reckoned that bird did that. He told me it was just its nature.[23]

As you continue your ministry, whenever the thought "If I had just known/done/been" drives you to peck a crack in the glass, know that what you are learning just might already be changing your nature and the nature of your church.

We celebrate you! Grace Abounds.

DAY 99

God is Still Calling You

Final words about final words. (Page 130)

THE PROPHETIC VOICE OF Isaiah speaks words we who seek to serve God in the church need to hear over and over again. They are written for God's people in community. However, today I invite you to read them for your own self, putting your own name into the text, even as you offer yourself to God, one more time.

But now thus says the Lord, who created you, O _____, who formed you _____, Do not fear, for I have redeemed you; I have called you by name, you are mine. When you pass through the waters, I will be with you; and through the rivers, they shall not overwhelm you; when you walk through fire you shall not be burned, and the flame shall not consume you. For I am the Lord your God, the Holy One of Israel, your Savior. I give Egypt as your ransom, Ethiopia and Seba in exchange for you. Because you are precious in my sight, and honored, and I love you. (Isaiah 43:1–4)

_____

_____

_____

_____

_____

_____

DAY 100

I Believe in You!

The Lord bless you and keep you,
　May the sun of many days shine through any darkness,
　　May the peace of Christ fill you,
　　　May your wisdom always grow and be shared
　　　　May grace, joy and love abide with you always.

Amen.

_____

_____

_____

_____

_____

_____

_____

Notes

DAY 1

1. Thomas Merton, *Thoughts in Solitude* (New York: Farrar, Straus & Cudahay, 1958), vii.

DAY 2

2. Tony Kushner, *Angels in America,* produced by Theatre Communications Group, New York.

DAY 7

3. The "swamp model" is presented more fully as a metaphor for one of the cultural models introduced in *How to Get Along with Your Church* in another book by George B. Thompson, Jr., *Alligators in the Swamp: Power, Leadership and Ministry* (Cleveland, Ohio: Pilgrim Press, 2005).

DAY 11

4. This unpublished prayer was prayed by Walter Bruegemann at the beginning of a Doctor of Ministry class at Columbia Theological Seminary in 1996. It was tape-recorded along with class notes for the day.

DAY 13

6. Tex Sample, *Ministry in an Oral Culture: Living with Will Rogers, Uncle Remus and Minnie Pearl* (Louisville: Westminster/John Knox Press, 1994).

DAY 14

6. The Center for Contemplative Dialogue is a not-for-profit organization focusing on reconciliation and understanding. Its founder and director is Steven Wirth. More information on contemplative dialogue can be found at the Web site: centerforcontemplativedialogue.org

DAY 18

7. Annie Dillard, *Teaching a Stone to Talk* (New York: Harper-Collins, 1982).

DAY 23

8. George B. Thompson, *Futuring Your Church: Finding Your Vision and Making It Work* (Cleveland: United Church Press, 1999). This book can become the "recipe book" for your church's vision statement. It provides an intentional step-by-step process for not only writing your vision but making it work.

DAY 41

9. John Heider, *The Tao of Leadership* (Atlanta: Humanics Limited, 1985).

DAY 42

10. Beverly (Thompson) Brigman, "Seeking God In the Midst of Transition" (D. Min. diss., Columbia Theological Seminary, 2000).

DAY 43

11. Trina Paulus, *Hope for the Flowers* (New York: Paulist Press, 1972), 76.

DAY 50

12. Renita J. Weems, *Listening for God: A Minister's Journey through Silence and Doubt* (New York: Simon and Schuster, 1999), 16.

DAY 55

13. Megan McKennan, *Not Counting Women and Children* (New York : Orbis, 2000), 15.

DAY 65

14. Parker Palmer, *Let Your Life Speak: Listening for the Voice of Vocation* (San Francisco: Jossey Bass, 2000), 54.

DAY 66

15. Reuben P. Job, *A Guide to Retreat for All God's Shepherds* (Nashville: Abingdon Press, 1994), 63.

DAY 67

16. Mark Lau Branson, *Memories, Hopes and Conversations: Appreciative Inquiry and Congregational Change* (Herndon: The Alban Institute, 2004), 137.

DAY 74

17. Eric Law, *The Wolf Shall Dwell with the Lamb: A Spirituality for Leadership in a Multicultural Community* (St. Louis: Chalice Press, 1993), chap. 9.

DAY 78

18. George B. Thompson, Sr., "Come, Rest a While," words and music written and sung, unpublished. Used by permission.

DAY 79

19. George B. Thompson, Jr. *Treasures in Clay Jars: New Ways to Understand Your Church* (Cleveland: The Pilgrim Press, 2003), chap. 1.

DAY 81

20. Steven Wirth, The Center for Contemplative Dialogue, workbook available online. See information regarding the ladder of inference.

DAY 82

21. George B., Thompson, Jr., ed., *Alligators in the Swamp: Power, Ministry, and Leadership* (Cleveland: The Pilgrim Press, 2005).

DAY 98

22. Rick Bragg, *All Over But The Shoutin'* (New York: Vintage Books, 1997), xi.